FREDERIC REMINGTON'S
Own Outdoors

FREDERIC REMINGTON'S

Own Outdoors

Written and Illustrated by

FREDERIC REMINGTON

With an Introduction by
HAROLD McCRACKEN

Edited by
DOUGLAS ALLEN

THE DIAL PRESS

1964   New York

Pictures on pages 164, 180-181, and 190 are used by
courtesy of Peter A. Juley and Son, New York, N. Y.

MANUFACTURED IN THE UNITED STATES OF AMERICA

Contents

Introduction

Frederic Remington was a man of many facets. Known as the foremost documentary artist of the Old West, he was extremely proficient in every artistic medium—pen-and-ink, pastels and oils—in addition to being an accomplished sculptor. He was, besides, a writer of considerable accomplishment in the fields of both fact and fiction. *Frederic Remington's Own Outdoors* introduces Remington the sportsman of wide and varied interests, both as writer and as artist.

Frederic Remington was very much a man's man. As a youngster he was far more interested in swimming and horseback riding than in learning his lessons. In his days at Yale University he won fame as a member of the varsity football team, together with the great Walter Camp, and as a heavyweight boxer, rather than as a scholar. A few years later, before he gained recognition as an artist, he seriously considered becoming a professional boxer to compete for the heavyweight championship. Always an expert horseman, Remington learned to handle a lasso with the dexterity of a cowboy. He was an enthusiastic outdoorsman by nature and preference, and hunting and fishing were as natural to him as drawing and painting. During the years between 1880 and the early 1900's which he spent adventuring, sketching and searching for scenes for his paintings, from the snowy forests of Canada to the arid regions of Old Mexico, Remington hunted for about every variety of big and small game in the American West—and remember these were the days of the big cattle roundups, when a lot of Indians were still using a scalping knife.

Frederic Remington's Own Outdoors shows the manly side of Remington's character and emphasizes the virile nature of his work as an artist of the Old West—a characteristic very few artists indeed share with him.

——Harold McCracken

9

Preface

On October 4, 1961, a postage stamp was issued to commemorate the one hundredth anniversary of the birth of Frederic Remington, the second time he had been so honored. No other American artist has had this distinction. As a part of this stamp's design there appeared the legend "Artist Of The Old West." Here was final justification of his position in American art, for he was indeed the Artist of the Old West and he is deservedly known for just that.

Many people, however, are not aware that he was a great sculptor and a fine writer as well. Nor are most people who are acquainted with his western works aware that Remington was a great portrayer of the sporting theme, one of the best of his time. While other artists were known for special activity in this field, he was diversified in his range and it is of no great wonder for the man was a sportsman to the core. He played on this in his stories as well as his illustrations.

The stories he told were true and invariably he was in all of them. It seems strange that this facet of the man's character appears to have been almost completely overlooked. Little of this phase of Remington's life has been written. His assignments carried him into Mexico where he told of hunting the peccary, into Canada's wilderness for caribou and moose, and into the Rockies for grizzly. He wrote of his days spent in the wheat fields of the Dakotas, coursing the "jack" in Kansas and pursuing the Blue Quail in the cactus country of the Rio Grande. He told of the rushing rivers and beautiful lakes of the northlands where great fish abounded. He was called upon to illustrate numerous articles and books, from bull-fighting in the country south of the border to tarpon fishing in Florida's waters. His drawings of the horse in sport were among the finest of his time for he was known as the man who "Knew the Horse."

These sporting scenes and sketches are all Remington with the exception of Julian Ralph's "Antoine's Moose-Yard," which has been inserted because Remington is a principal character and this story adds to the sporting story of his life, and "Remington on Tiger Hunting" because of its humorous aspects.

I do not presume on this book as part of a biography—it is autobiography. Any remarks I have made are intended only to broaden the background of the writing and illustration he did so well.

It is good that Remington's star rested in his portrayal of the Old West for without this much of our heritage would have been lost. There was little that the camera could do to catch the spirit of it. It is also good that he was a great sportsman as well for he left us much here also.

It seems to me not so strange that Remington's first published story was one on sport—"Coursing Rabbits on the Plains," and that the first Remington prints to appear were—"Antelope Hunting" and "Goose Shooting," published in 1889.

It is my wish to acknowledge with gratitude the help and encouragement I received from some who are among us and some who have passed on—the late E. Walter Latendorf, Charlie Everett and Mahonri Young. To Helen Card, Dr. Harold McCracken and Tom Lea. To my family especially who encouraged me in my collecting and writing.

——DOUGLAS ALLEN

FREDERIC REMINGTON IN THE UNIFORM OF THE DAY: CANVAS JACKET
AND FLANNEL TROUSERS

Football Days at Yale

I SHOULD ALWAYS HAVE REMEMBERED Remington without his rising to fame, for a little wrestling match in which we once indulged resulting in my receiving a broken shoulder blade, a broken collar bone and a dislocation of the arm."[1]

These were the reminiscenses of one Julian Wilder, a cadet and fellow classmate at the Highland Military Academy in Worcester, Massachusetts, where Remington spent a portion of his youth learning the ways of the military. It was also descriptive of the boy who, as another student put it, "was vital, aggressive and full of good humor."[2]

And so it was that this "vital and aggressive" youth of seventeen came out of the St. Lawrence country in the fall of 1878 to study art at Yale University in New Haven, Connecticut. It was, however, another activity which made young Frederic Remington far better known at Yale than his desire to draw and paint. This was the game of football which was then in its very infancy, the first inter-collegiate game having been played between Princeton and Rutgers just ten years before. Remington took to football immediately for here was a perfect outlet for his exuberant nature and its demand for sheer strength. He became devoted to it with a passion that was characteristic of him.

It wasn't until his return to the campus in the fall of 1879 that he be-

[1] Orin Edson Crooker, "A Page from the Boyhood of Frederic Remington," *Collier's,* September 17, 1910.
[2] *Op. cit.*

13

came a regular member of the varsity. This team was notable if for no other reason than it had as its captain a young student, Walter Camp, who in future years did so much to make the game what it is today and who has long been recognized as the "Father of Football." The game as played in 1879 had little semblance to the game as it is played today. As with any new thing it had to develop and grow. It was a time of experiment. There was little in the way of coaching. This is evidenced by the following.

Camp's room served as the quarters for discussions and the players came in the long autumn evenings to sit around on the floor and go over plays and the other things of importance that centered around the game. John Harding, who played a forward position on the team, related some of these incidents.

"During my last two years of football the 'rushers' were unanimously of the opinion that the kicking, dodging and passing game was the game we should strive for and it was the duty of the half-back and backs to end their runs with a good long punt, wherever possible, and give us a chance to get under the ball when it came down, while the rest of the team behind the line were in favor of a running mass play game, particularly in wet and slippery weather.

"I remember once in my senior year our divergence of views on this question, about three weeks before the final game, nearly split our team. Camp, fearful of wet weather and possible snow at the Thanksgiving game, with Channing, Eaton and Fred Remington as the heavy Yale ends, and everybody 'big' in the rush line excepting myself, was trying to develop us with as little kicking as possible, and was sensitive because of the protests from the rush line that there was no kicking. We were all summoned one evening to his [Camp's] room in Durfee.

"When all were gathered, Camp put the issue directly before the team. He expressed his unwillingness to remain the captain unless his ideas were adhered to, as he felt that all due things considered his plan was the safer course to follow. Things were eventually smoothed out to the mutual satisfaction of all concerned."[3]

The game was played with fifteen men on each side. The Yale Banner of 1880 published the following roster for the team of 1879.

FORWARDS —F. M. Eaton, J. S. Harding, L. K. Hull, B. B. Lamb, H. H. Knapp, J. Moorehead, F. Remington, C. S. Beck.

HALFBACKS —W. I. Badger, W. C. Camp, G. H. Clark, W. A. Peters, R. W. Watson.

BACKS —W. W. K. Nixon, C. W. Lyman.

SUBSTITUTES—B. W. Bacon, F. R. Vernon, J. S. Durand, J. F. Merrill, C. B. Storrs.

[3] William H. Edwards, *Football Days*, Moffat Yard and Company, New York, N.Y., 1916.

This is quite different from the teams fielded today when fifty or so men stream onto the stadium turf for each side. Here were fifteen men and five substitutes to play a game which was rough in the extreme and with few holds barred.

The game all Yale men looked forward to in those days, as well as today, was the encounter with Princeton. In this year of 1879 the game was scheduled for Thanksgiving Day morning, November 27th. Yale had enjoyed a successful season, having defeated Rutgers, Columbia and Pennsylvania. They had tied Harvard. The part that Remington played in these games has not been recorded to my knowledge. Coverage of the game in those days was sketchy and any play was given to the backs much as it is now. The linemen rarely received the notices of the press. Yale was determined to take the title away from Princeton who had won it from them the year before. This loss, they knew, was their own doing because laxness in training and attitude had become prevalent among some of the members of the squad who felt that they could beat any competition with little effort.

This Thanksgiving Day game was played at the St. George Cricket Club in Hoboken, New Jersey. It was a fair geographical traveling point for both teams and an ideal location to hold the contest. Some consternation was felt since the weather report indicated that the day would be cold and cloudy with rain in the afternoon. The rain did not materialize.

The Jersey City *Argus*, November 28, 1879 quotes, "From early morning the city was entirely (we presume this meant Hoboken) deserted. Nearly all the clubs, engine, military and target companies and associations going out of town. If Hoboken was deserted by its own, this was more than counteracted, however, by the influx of visitors from New York and elsewhere who came in droves to witness the great match. It is estimated that over six thousand persons were present inside the grounds and fully four thousand viewed the struggle from the roofs of stages, express wagons and house tops in the neighborhood.

"The game was both exciting and interesting, the Princeton boys coming within a few feet at one time of winning a goal. Several scrimmages occurred during the play and the most intense and bitter feeling was displayed in several instances. Two of the Princeton men and one of the Yale men were injured accidentally during the game which was called a draw, time being called about five o'clock and before either side had scored a goal."

The crowds gathered along the roped off area and stands, a colorful foreground to the multi-hued autumn display on the heights rising beyond. Mr. A. B. Frost, a noted illustrator for many years, drew a picture of one of the scenes from this game and it was originally reproduced in *Harper's Weekly*, December 29, 1879. It is again reproduced here and the Yale

FOOTBALL MATCH BETWEEN YALE AND PRINCETON

16

player shown on the left of the picture with his elbow blocking a Princeton man looks very much as if he might be Frederic Remington.

Remington did not return to Yale after the Christmas holidays. It will never be known where his position in the history of Yale football would have been if he had remained. His going eventually proved extremely important to himself and to future generations of Americans for it inadvertantly proved to be the turning point in his life. It was also football's gain for not too many years later Remington painted and had published one of the first fine football pictures of players in action. It was entitled "A Tackle and Ball Down," and appeared on the cover of *Harper's Weekly*, November 26, 1887. There followed for the same publication "A Practice Game at Yale," "A Collision at the Ropes," "A Day With the Yale Team," and "A Run Behind Interference." All are reproduced on these pages. The pictures portrayed a chronological period in the early development of the game and with Remington's gift for drawing action and his insistence for detail and accuracy, they prove valuable to the students of that period.

In 1894, Walter Camp, Remington's old captain, was approached to compile data and statistics on football. This action resulted from pressure and criticism on the part of non-participants who felt the game savage in its aspects and not fit to be called a sport or to be played by young men of good breeding.

Mr. Camp felt that the men who could and would vouch for the game were those who had played it. Many of these had made their mark in life and were highly respected citizens. The result of this compilation of data and statistics was published by Harper & Brothers in 1894 under the title *Football Facts and Figures*. In this little book the following letter is printed:

New Rochelle, N. Y.
April 3, 1894

Let the good work go on—but who the devil is making all this trouble? They are not going to pass any state law on it I hope. Football, in my opinion, is best at its worst—to be Irish. I do not believe in all this namby-pamby talk and I hope the game will not be emasculated and robbed of its heroic qualities, which is its charm and its destructive quality. People who do not like football as now played might like whist—advise them to try that.

Yours faithfully,
Frederic Remington

Many years later an old team mate F. R. Vernon eulogized, "Frederic Remington was a member of our team. We were close friends and spent many Sunday afternoons on long walks. I can see him now with his India ink pencil sketching as we went along, and I must laugh now at the nerve I had to joke him about his efforts. Remy was a good football player and one of the best boxers in college."

"A TACKLE AND A BALL DOWN"

This is the first of the Remington football illustrations to be published. The Yale team of 1887 was fortunate in having several players who were outstanding and who had tremendous effect upon the younger players coming up, players who would carry on the tradition of the game for the next few years and form the nucleus of teams which could lay claim to some of the greatest players of the old era. The names of George Woodruff, Bill Bull and Pa Corbin will forever be remembered by Yale men. This illustration appeared on the cover of *Harper's Weekly*, November 26, 1887.

A Low Tackle   The Drop-Kick   Heeling a Fair Catch   A Low Runner

Brushing Off   The Place-Kick for Goal   A Long Pass

"A PRACTICE GAME AT YALE"

The great team of 1888 is pictured by Remington in the all important practice session. This was a daily routine with strict emphasis placed on the fundamentals of tackling and kicking, the latter being much more a part of the game than it is today. This team had an array of players which the sentimental think unequaled in the annals of football. Walter Camp considered it the greatest of all time, which meant at least up until 1923. Their guard, Pudge Heffelfinger, was considered the fastest big man football had ever seen and at fifty-three scrimmaged with the college boys. He died at the age of eighty-seven. And then there was Charlie Gill, Tom McClung, Corbin and Rhodes. There, also, was that grand old man of football, Amos Alonzo Stagg. Many is the player alive today who was taught the rudiments of the sport by this outstanding member of the '88 team. This picture appeared in *Harper's Weekly*, November 24, 1888.

"COLLISION AT THE ROPES"

The Thanksgiving Day game of 1890 pitted Yale against Princeton for the title. Thus the two met again in an uninterrupted string that went back to 1878 when Yale had joined the College Football Association whose members were Harvard, Columbia and Princeton.

Yale started her season of 1890 poorly but came along strong at the end to defeat Princeton 32 to 0. The illustration depicts a scene from this game and appeared in *Harper's Weekly*, November 29, 1890.

A Good Tackle

The Cock Crows

After the Snap-Back

Football Armor

Blocking

Rubbing Down in the Gymnasium

A Bit of Advice

"A DAY WITH THE YALE TEAM"

Remington, in the company of Richard Harding Davis, traveled to New Haven one morning to watch the Yale team go through its daily routine and to renew old acquaintance with the coach and his former captain, Walter Camp. The events were recorded in this illustration but not before Remington had been reminded of an old story . . . "of how he dipped his jacket in a pool of blood at the slaughter house to make it look more businesslike."

He wondered why, after so many traditions and landmarks had passed away, that this particular story should alone survive to rise up out of the past to confront him. Reproduced in *Harper's Weekly*, November 18, 1893.

"A RUN BEHIND INTERFERENCE"

The title of this picture is all that the name implies. It illustrates the legendary flying wedge upon point of contact. This offensive was so dangerous that it was later outlawed. It can readily be understood what the results of this type of play must have been when such names as Butterworth, Adee, Hickok and Hinkey opposed Wheeler, Lea, Trenchard and King—Yale and Princeton immortals. This illustration appeared in *Harper's Weekly*, December 2, 1893.

Remington's year at Yale had a profound effect on the course his future was to take. It was during this period that he became acquainted with two young men who in some measure were responsible for this. One was a fellow art student, Poultney Bigelow, the other, Robert Camp, not to be confused with Remington's former football captain, Walter Camp.

During the years between December 1879 and 1883 he and Camp kept in touch with each other. Camp was graduated from Yale in 1882 and returned home to Milwaukee. He heard about sheep ranching in Kansas and decided that here lay his destiny. Enthused at the life, he suggested in a letter that Remington purchase a property adjoining his that was available. In the early spring of 1883 Remington left Canton for the west and sheep ranching. It was not long before Remington met two young men occupied in the same endeavor. Their names were James Chapman and an Englishman referred to in the record as Charlie B. The foursome became inseparable and on occasion Remington's ranch hand, Bill Kehr, and a newly settled rancher, John Mitchner joined the foursome—life on the Kansas prairie could be a lonesome one.

A year of ranching and Remington lost his enthusiasm, sold his stake and in the spring of 1884 headed for the southwest. In the late summer of 1884 he returned to Kansas, settled in Kansas City and began painting from the sketches he had made during the previous months. It was at this time that he was conned into investing a good portion of his money as a partner in an emporium and lost it just as fast. Discouraged and lonely, just twenty-three, he returned east and married the girl who had been waiting for him—Eva Caten. The two returned to Kansas and settled in the house he still owned there. Remington again set about to paint from his sketches and forwarded them to eastern publications as fast as he turned them out. One of these was accepted and published by *Harper's Weekly* but only after it had been redrawn by another artist—"Ejecting An Oklahoma Boomer"; drawn by T. de Thulstrup from a sketch by Frederic Remington, March 28, 1885. And this was it. For the young couple it was a constant struggle. It was best that Eva return home. Once again Remington was drawn to the Southwest. In the summer of 1885 he returned to Kansas City laden with a portfolio of sketches, settled his accounts, and returned to New York. Eva met him there and they once more settled down. This time he trudged from publisher to publisher.

One of these was the House of Harper's, publishers of the popular *Harper's Weekly* who had produced one of Remington's drawings earlier that year. Mr. Henry Harper saw that the drawings he now presented "were very crude, but had all the ring of new and live material."[4]

On January 9, 1886 there appeared "The Apache War: Indian Scouts On Geronimo's Trail," and during the balance of that year nine more drawings were accepted and published in *Harper's Weekly*.

This good fortune did not constitute stability but it did acknowledge the fact that Remington's work was recognized by one of the great publishers of the day.

It was during this time that Remington walked into the Morse Building at Nassau Street and Newspaper Row, made his way to the attic of the building and entered the office of the *Outing* Magazine.

"One day in the *Outing* office I was hard at work making up a forthcoming number, and correspondingly irritable at any interruption . . . when I was again interrupted by a vast portfolio held in the hands of some intruding one, of course I knew that this meant looking at some drawings, and probably turning away some artist who needed money, and needed still more the qualities that make success.

"Feeling cross and weary, I did not even look up at the huge visitor, but held out a hand for the drawings. He pushed one at me and it was as though he had given me an electric shock. Here was the real thing, the unspoiled native genius dealing with Mexican ponies, cowboys, cactus, lariats and sombreros. No stage heroes these; no carefully pomaded hair and neatly tied cravats; these were

[4] J. Henry Harper, *The House of Harper*, 1912.

the men of the real rodeo, parched in alkali dust, blinking out from barely opened eyelids under the furious rays of an Arizona sun. I had been there, and my innermost corpuscles vibrated at the truth before me. I looked at the signature—Remington. There was nothing, however, to suggest the work of my homonymous fellow-student of Yale.

"I was delighted at my discovery, and said to him, 'It's an odd coincidence, I had a classmate at Yale . . .' but before I could add another word out he roared: 'Hell! Big—is that you?'

"He had turned himself into a cowboy and I had become slave to a desk. We embraced; we made so much noise that my colleagues in the outer office feared that a fight was on. I introduced all present and then pulled forth from pigeon-holes every manuscript likely to interest such a pencil. Anything that might serve as an excuse for introducing horses, cowboys, army types and frontier background was eagerly sought, and as fervently welcomed by my quondam classmate. He was bankrupt in purse. *Outing* was also bankrupt, but did not realize it. Every great magazine of New York had turned him away from the desk of the so-called art editor, because forsooth none of these orthodox picture buyers could see anything good in a horse that had not been groomed or a soldier in shirtsleeves. But genius was in those rough drawings, and I loved them for their very roughness. Of course I bought out all he had in his portfolio, and I loaded him with orders likely to keep him in every number of the magazine for two or three years."[5]

Thus it was that Poultney Bigelow described in his own words his meeting with Remington after so many years. It was for *Outing* Magazine that there appeared in the May 1887 issue Remington's first story "Coursing Rabbits On The Plains"—reminiscences of his former life on the Kansas prairie with Bob Camp, James Chapman and the young Englishman Charlie B.

[5] Poultney Bigelow, *Seventy Summers,* 1925, I, 303-305.

Coursing Rabbits On The Plains

LOOK HERE, BOYS, what do you say to running 'jacks' tomorrow?" said Jim, as he brought his chair down from its canted back position against the wall of the room, and, by way of an emphasizer, striking the table a blow with his fist which made the little kerosene lamp dance a jig.

I seconded the motion immediately, but Bob, the owner of the ranch, sat back and reflectively sucked his big pipe, as he thought of the things which ought to be done. The broken fence to the corral down by the creek, dredging the watering holes, the possibilities of trading horses down at Plum Grove and various other thrifty plans weighed upon his mind; but Jim continued—"It's nice fall weather now, dry and cold; why, a hoss will jest run hisself to death for fun; that old Bob mule scampered like a four year ole colt all the way to Hoyt's with me to-day, and, besides, there hain't nothing to do, and the 'jacks' is thicker'n tumbleweeds on the prairie."

The sporting blood began to mount to Robert's great, contemplative eyes as the arguments went home; so removing his pipe he blew the smoke upwards as sedately as Irving's Dutchmen, shook off his Van Twiller doubts and declared he was an enthusiast, as indeed he was when he had made up his mind.

"That settles it," gleefully shouted Jim, "old Push-Bob (his horse) can have the bit to-morrow. Come here, Peggy, old son." Out from the corner

27

behind the stove sneaked a dog and approached Jim in a delighted, side-long, apologetic way, which gave the cue to his cur blood.

"I say, Jim, you hain't agoin' to make Peg-Leg run hisself to death over these yar prairies, be you?" came from Phip, the cook, as he put away the supper dishes. "Ha-ha," he laughed; "poor old Peg-Leg: he never seed a Jack-rabbit 'cept the rabbit were a'disappearin' down the horizon like a fallin' star. Peg's a right smart good dog to run these yar land turtles with, but Peg hain't much account a'runnin' of jacks."

"Never you mind," replied the chivalric James, whose large nature always went out to the inferior and oppressed, "Peg ain't no sprint-runner fer a fact, but if them spider-dogs (meaning the grey-hounds) misses bunny, old Peg gets them before the sun goes down," and patting Peg-Leg encouragingly, "Well, go lay and rest yerself; that's a good dog." And Peg-Leg sneaked back to the obscurity of the cook-stove. Peg-Leg was not a grey-hound, nor indeed was he a fox-hound, although he was called such by persons not accurate on dog matters. He had lost the symmetry of one forward leg at some time during puphood and had been christened after the Indian fashion from his peculiarity, Peg-Leg. Peg was not a good coursing dog, but after the fashion of his breed, he always caught his rabbit. He ran at a limping gallop, but his nose was a most sensitive organ, and when on a trail he had a tenacity of purpose which was nearly canine insanity. He was, besides, on personal friendly relations with all us boys, and attended our hunts from what I suppose was a sense of duty, as he certainly could not have enjoyed them, considering that he was along tailing behind the fast hounds and bounding horses; but should the rabbit make a sharp crook and get away in some bad bit of country, we only had to wait until Peg-Leg came up and showed us the way he had gone. The jack-rabbit does not run far at one time, although his break away is in-describable except as a disappearing shadow, but Peg would manage to rout him out again.

The next preliminary was to enlist John S———— in the scheme, for he owned the grey-hounds, so I was deputized to go and see Johnny as I rode away to my home down the creek.

"Hark! didn't I hear horses?" ejaculated Phip, as he stopped at the open door after discharging a pan of dish-water into the outer darkness. "Yes, and comin' like mad."

We all went to the door and listened a moment, when James retired to his chair and began to roll a fresh cigarette with the remark, "It's that crazy Englishman; no one but a ———— fool would ride like that on a dark night." For when the clatter, clatter of the horse's hoofs stopped in front of the house and a big red face was thrust into the room with the greeting, " 'Ello, bies," one could immediately see that Charlie B—— was not as Jim had described him.

"Come in, Charlie; tie yer hoss to the corral and come in," was Bob's return greeting, whereat Charlie disappeared.

"That chap 'ill go hunting," said the practical Phip, sententiously, as he chuckled away, and poked at the fire; "it's a cold day when that Englishman won't go hunting, or any where else where there hain't no work ter do." We realized the force of this, and Charlie verified it by declaring that he was delighted with the prospect when he had come in from outside.

Charlie B——— was your typical country Englishman, and the only thing about him American was the broncho he rode. He was the best fellow in the world, cheery, hearty and ready for a lark at any time of the day or night. He owned a horse ranch seven miles down the creek, and found visiting his neighbors involved considerable riding; but Charlie was a sociable soul, and did not appear to mind that, and he would spend half the night riding over the lonely prairies to drop in on a friend in some neighboring ranch, in consequence of which Charlie's visits were not always timely; but he seemed never to realize that a chap was not in as good condition to visit when awakened from his blanket at three o'clock in the morning as in the twilight hour.

" 'Ose going, Bob?" he asked.

"Well, let's see;" and Bob surveyed the company. "There's Jim and Fred, and you and myself and Johnnie S———; and Bill Carr will want to go, won't he, Fred?"

"Yes. Bill will want to give old Prince a whirl, and Prince will want to be whirled; for do you know what, that old, grey, sleepy plug never wakes up and acts like a horse unless he sees a 'jack' in front of him"; and by way of peroration I added, "He never saw a horse there."

As I had expected, this stirred up the horse question, which commanded all the intellect, the interest, the finer feelings and the subtle jealousies of the cow-camps. The exact running qualities of the horses were debatable, and every new horse that came into the White-water bottoms had to cost its owner a couple of snug bets in order to find out that Prince and Push-Bob could beat him. But whether Prince or Push-Bob were the best was an active subject of conjecture, and one which we never tired of. Jim immediately indulged in some sage doubts on my reflections on Prince, and we all laughed as James began to nerve up for a storm.

"Don't stir up that yar horse question or you'll have Jim a bettin' more money in this ole shanty than the Sante Fe road could put up," came from Phip, who was one of your intellectual horsemen, not given to betting, but taking a more sensible view; "still," he continued, "that 'ar Prince is as good as anybody's horse 'cept fer that heavy for'd leg, but then Push he's a right smart sort of a plug hisself—"

"Hold on, Phip, thought you didn't want the horse question," came from another corner, and Phip laughed, subsided and poked the fire in silence.

"What are you going to ride, Charlie?" was asked.

"The blue mare—the big un's gone lame in 'is stifle of late; think the bloody mules must have landed 'im one on 'is joint; but the little blue mare's a good 'n, she's a good 'oss. I'll show ye fellows a fine pair of 'ind 'oofs to-morrow," and Charlie slapped his boots with his whip and smiled triumphantly.

"I suppose the little yaller gal will have to take it to-morrow," said Jim, as he gazed humorously at my one hundred eighty pounds avoirdupois.

"Yes," I replied; "Terra-Cotta and I'll try and keep up with the procession."

"Bob, there, 'e'll ride that black vagabond of 'is, 'e'll go in partnership with what's 'is name 'ere—Peg-Leg," bantered Charlie.

Bob allowed that if old Jane felt like it, he would distinguish himself, but he added: "I expect she's located out there on the prairie and I'll have to send in to the ranch for a pair of mules," referring to a propensity of his favorite mare to balk; "but if she don't, I am not hunting sympathy, fer I won't need it."

So the evening passed pleasantly amid boyish banter, and the horse talk so dear to the stockman's heart. Presently, finding the hour to be late, B——— and I bade the boys on Bob's ranch good night, went out, bestrode our horses and rode off down the creek to our homes. Passing Johnnie S———'s ranch, we pounded a reveille on the door, which presently brought the owner to it, rubbing his eyes and inquiring "What the —— we wanted in the middle of the night? Oh! it's you, is it, B———? Well, I might know. Say, B———, what's the matter with the daytime for calling on a fellow?"

We explained that our visit would be short, disclosed our plans, and expatiated on the joys of "jack" running, and finally Johnnie concluded that the interests of his cows required that he run "jacks" on the morrow; so we rode off and left him to his slumbers. Johnnie was an important adjunct, as he owned the grey-hounds, but now that his cooperation was assured, everything was ready for the sport. At last I was snug in bed, and B——— was presumably in his somewhat later, though it mattered little as to that, considering his personal habits. Poor B———! later on, his remittances from the old country stopped, and the last I heard of that lump of generous nature he was working for the man who owned his ranch, and keeping better hours in the interest of his employer.

I mention these preliminaries to allow the reader to become interested in the horses which were to do the running, as "jack" coursing is a succession of sharp quarter or half mile dashes, generally run in a clump, and well adapted to the spry little broncho horses, who would cut a sorry figure in a

long English fox chase; and then this neat little sport is generally practiced
by the ranchmen and farmers of the west, and while not exactly an event
in our lives, yet it was a day spent apart from the usual duties, and therefore interesting.

I ate a light breakfast, and indeed the ranch larder helped me to do
that; and after a feed of oats, rubbed Terra-Cotta down, and then put a
light saddle on in place of my heavy stock saddle weighing some thirty-
five pounds. Terra-Cotta was a nervous little half-breed Texas and
thoroughbred, of a beautiful light gold-dust color, with a Naples yellow
color mane and tail. She always knew that the light saddle meant a sharp
run, and her fiery little thoroughbred nature asserted itself. In a moment
she was in a te-he, and could scarcely wait for me to mount, but was off
in a gallop before I was finally seated. Bill, my ranch hand, followed me on
old Prince, and the gallop across the prairie to Bob's was glorious. The light
haze hung over the plains, not yet dissipated by the rising sun. Terra-
Cotta's stride was steel springs under me as she swept along, brushing the
dew from the grass of the range and taking the bit smartly in her teeth
as though to say, "Come on, let's have a run," but I pulled gently and
coaxed her to save herself for a later hour. Off to the right we saw another
figure going toward Bob's, and in a few moments, by converging, found
Johnnie S——— mounted on his big bay and leading one grey-hound.

"Good morning, Johnnie, where is the other dog?"

"She thought she would stay at home to-day—you see, the old lady has
expectations, and—well, it's good judgment on her part. But here's Daddy,
and he's good for all the jack-rabbits on the range."

Later on we came up with Charlie B——— on the blue mare, and rigged
out in full English hunting tog, all except a red coat, which is an addition
not generally appreciated in the western country.

On over the smiling reach of grass, grown dry and sere in the August
suns and hot winds, we galloped four abreast. The boys had on light saddles
and snaffle bits, and while Mr. B——— sported a hunting stock, the rest
contented themselves with light poles some six feet long, which were to
be used as lances, with which to touch the rabbit, a feat most difficult and
improbable. We all had discarded our chaparajos, and the horses were
lightly blanketed. The rise and fall of the perfect lope peculiar to the
American broncho was observable in all its ease and beauty. The blue mare
looked blue indeed. She was one of those freaks of color which one sees
occasionally on the plains. Johnnie's bay horse was a powerful animal, and
a pleasant horse to get along with. Johnnie and he had a perfect understanding, and never seemed to clash. It made no difference to the horse on which
part of his back Johnnie was, he attended strictly to his own business. Terra
is already known, but now glance at Prince. You would not think him a
quarter-horse, for he looks like a clumsy, sleepy old plug. Iron grey, with no

AND ON OVER THE RANGE

flesh and big bones, he moves powerfully, steadily, but "where is the snap?" you will say. Oh, it's there, somewhere, and always comes out on occasion. Many a man associates wealth that is gone with the name of Prince, and many a quarter-horse has found his Waterloo as he has followed old Prince over the scratch; still he is not much of a horse to look at, and that is a strong point, because the other fellows always went their last dollar on appearances.

After a few moments' ride we drew rein in Bob C——'s corral and went into the house, where the boys were eating their breakfasts.

"Do you know, old Phip has got waked up and wants to run jacks, so he's going to lower his dignity and take a spurt on Bob," explained Jim.

We all laughed, for we knew Phip was an eminently practical person, who had rarely spared time for trivial things, and had neglected to learn in his studious career to ride a horse. Furthermore, we knew "Bob." "Bob" was a mule, somewhat advanced in years, but with his character yet unformed, as it were. At least, those who were charitable toward the mule said this, but I think he was bad and malicious. Of course he had spells of goodness, but even a mule must rest for crime; in the main, though, he was sulky, was known to bite, was believed capable of kicking, was grossly given to bucking, and perfectly certain to balk; and the only thing he

32

would not do was to run away, and that is a virtue in a hunting horse. "Bob" had at various times elevated some of the best riders in that part of the country toward the stars, but Phip was incredulous, and had evolved a theory that the base of Bob's character was good, and that all he needed was intelligent handling, etc., all of which will appear later on.

"Jim, do you want to gaunt Peg-Leg for a race, or will you give him his ration?" grinned Phip, as he held up the remains of breakfast on a plate, which Peg-Leg was regarding with fixed and intelligent gaze.

"Oh, give him his grub—he don't exercise violently when he runs; if he don't start on a full stomach he'll starve to death before he can catch a 'jack'." This brought breakfast and contentment to Peg-Leg.

The horses were saddled, and all being mounted, Phip included, the cavalcade moved out of the corral, up the bluffs and on over the range.

"I'm going to watch Push-Bob and Prince to-day to see where the money is," whispered Johnnie to me as we rode ahead. The horses were all fretful and uneasy, except old Prince, whose great good sense always told him when the hour had come. Even old Jane, Bob's mare, condescended to take an interest and manifest a disposition to pound sod, which was exceedingly gratifying to Robert, inasmuch as the condition of Jane's feelings were to be considered as to whether she would go or not. Jane was not a plug, be it understood, but a good American mare, with all the saddle gaits, but she was in the years of discretion, and had multiplied her race in various instances.

"Say, Jim, do you know ———"

"There's a jack—take him, Daddy," came a quick cry from Johnnie, and the next moment Johnnie's big bay was off. There goes the rabbit, the dog flies after. "Go on, Terra," I shouted, loosing on the bit, hitting her lightly with a spur, and away we went, all in a ruck. Old Prince was shouldering heavily away on my right, Push-Bob on my quarter, Jane off to the left, and Phip at a stately gallop behind—the blue mare being left at the post as it were.

The horses tore along, blowing great lung-fulls of fresh morning air out in snorts. Our sombreros blew up in front from the rush of air, and our blood leaped with excitement. Away scurried the jack, with his great ears sticking up like two antique bed-posts, with Daddy closing the distance rapidly, and our outfit thundering along some eight rods in the rear. Down into a slew of long grass into which the rabbit and dog disappeared we went, with the grass snapping and swishing about the legs of our horses. A dark mass on my left heaves up, and "ho—there goes Bob head over heels." On we go. "Hope Bob isn't hurt—must have put his foot into a water-hole," are my excited reflections. We are out of the slew, but where is the rabbit and dog?

"Here they go," comes from Phip, who is standing on the edge of the slew, farther down toward the bluffs of the bottoms, where he has gotten as the result of a short cut across.

Phip digs his spurs into the mule, sticks out his elbows and manifests other frantic desires to get there, all of it reminding one strongly of the style of one Ichabod Crane, but as we rush by, it is evident that the mule is debating a question with that assurance born of the consciousness that when the thing is brought to a vote he has a majority in the house. Poor Phip, now for your theories!

Up a rise in the draw onto the plain we go helter-skelter, over some stony land and then a nice level, with Mr. Jack-Rabbit twenty rods in the lead, and Daddy skirmishing along his wake. It is no use running now, he has too much of a start; so I pull in the impetuous Terra and I cut across to the left, hoping bunny will dodge that way, and of course, in the event that he does not, I am out of the race. Ah, just as I had expected, bunny had dodged, and Daddy whizzed by some two rods before he could feel his rudder and come about. The jack was bearing nearly on to me, with Daddy quite far behind. Terra sees it, I think, as I turn her head, shake the rein and whisper, "Go on, girl," and we are off. "Now go on, Terra; what are you good for?" I yelled, lifting her forward. I leaned over and extended my stick, but the jack is by two feet too far. A couple of jumps and—"There, I missed him. Whoa, Terra, you little fool; you want to run all over the prairie for nothing?"

The rabbit made back for the draw or ravine, considering the broken country as better than "a fair field and no favor." He kept doubling and throwing the dog off, for he was evidently old game. The draw was rough, stony, and the bed of the dry stream was filled with a thick growth of willows. By some good maneuvering, James got right on to him, and was going straight for the willows. The rabbit and dog shot through, and Jim gallantly followed on Push-Bob, for I verily believe that the horse would have charged a stone wall. As they struck the thick brush, Jim was swept from his seat like a fly from a sugar-bowl, and the horse went on.

After more running about, doubling and twisting, Charlie B——— and Bill C——— started in together, and as I stood in the draw dismounted, the rabbit, dog, Charlie and Bill swept over a little hill and full at me, with a regular, reckless "Cannon-on-the-right-of-them" swing. I leaped into the saddle as they came. Crash through the willows they went, and there came disaster. The bank was worn away on the other side by a cattle-path just wide enough for one. They were neck and neck, both ambitious to use the narrow path; so at it they rushed, and any philosopher will anticipate what befell them. They bunted rudely together, upsetting each horse and rider, while I galloped up the path between them with a cheer, leaving them rolling in a cloud of dust, and blaming each other. As accidents seemed to be the rule of the run, I helped out the rule in this wise: The bluffs which overlooked the White-water bottoms lay off to the left some forty rods, and toward them went the dog and rabbit, with me following pell-mell. I have since explained how it happened in some dozen odd ways, but at this distant day I do not seem to concur in any of my own explanations, so I have ceased laying the blame on Terra-Cotta, and taken upon my own shoulders the responsibility of riding full tilt right over the bluffs. When we arrived at the bluff, Terra-Cotta could not be stopped. The incline was about fifty degrees and well sodded, though lumpy, and Terra's knees bent under her at the first step downward, and others have said that we made the descent sandwich fashion, though the details are somewhat obscured. I lay on the ground for a moment, expecting to find a bone on a strike, or some blood running, but I did not, and so arose to find I was not hurt in the least. Terra got on her feet, shook herself and looked foolish. I took her by the bridle, saying, "Are you hurt, old girl?" As though to say "Not a bit," she turned about, and every muscle and bone answered its summons. The rabbit got away, and he had almost avenged his race in the ordeal, for upon assembling, Mr. Robert C——— presented himself in a guise which I can only compare to a sketch in plaster. Old Jane had put both forward legs into a slew-hole, and Mr. Robert was dumped in the mud. When we met he still carried a nice coating of slime and blue clay on his person, while old Jane was gradually growing white as the clay dried in the cool air that was blowing. She looked as though she thought her matronly dignity had been trifled with. We did not take these calamities to heart, but thought it a good opening for a day's sport.

Peg-Leg came up and sat on his haunches near our group, and looked sulkily at the far horizon as much as to say, "That's a nice way to hunt."

"Well, let's try it again! Come along up the draw. Come, Peggy, old boy," said Jim, as he led off at a fox trot. Johnnie had caught the grey-hound, and we were ready for another view. We drew up our girths and made up our minds that we would not let the next jack get such a start on us. We kept a sharp lookout, when suddenly Peggy barks and goes limping across the prairie on what will evidently be a lone hunt, as it is only a trail and no rabbit in sight.

"That's good day for Peg-Leg," laughs Jim. "Peg-Leg is abused, and I'll be hanged if I blame him for bein' disgusted—but he's got a hunt all to hisself now, so good luck to him."

We rode up the draw about a quarter of a mile and stopped for Johnnie to fix a cincha. He was long about it, and we sat on our horses and chatted. Off to the right about a third of a mile was Peg-Leg, nosing along with an occasional bark. We watched him when he gradually turned toward us.

"Peg's coming this way, and I wouldn't wonder if there was a jack somewhere in the grass, as it's long enough to hide one," remarked one.

THE JACK WAS BEARING NEARLY ONTO ME

"Jest mind your eye; I wouldn't wonder if Peg would start one, so look out," went on another, and the words were hardly out of his mouth before a jack of enormous size sprang up from right under Peg's nose, and like a rubber ball came bounding toward us.

"Hi, Johnnie, give Daddy the sight," we yelled.

Daddy got it and was off—we after. The rabbit was evidently only thinking of Peg-Leg, and was running right into the jaws of Daddy.

"There, we got him," we shouted, but, "no," for the jack had passed seemingly right under Daddy's body, was among our horses' feet the next moment, and gone in our rear before we could stop.

Phip, who was galloping in our rear, had his golden opportunity now, and got out his stick to deal the champion stroke, when the mule spying the rabbit coming toward him, shied violently and left Phip sprawling about on the grass. We had swept about with a wheel to the right and left, and were again on the trail. As we passed Phip, he was using some of the strongest parts of the Saxon language with very telling effect. We all laughed and passed on.

After a sharp run, Bill got near enough to the rabbit to deal a violent blow, which started the dust in a shower and broke his stick, but Charlie caught the rabbit on the turn, and with a backhand stroke he knocked what little life was left out of the bunny, and Daddy finished him.

Phip caught his mule and came up. He insisted that the mule was perverse beyond all rule and precedent, and passed without discussion some ironical remarks about "riding a horse" which were made by Robert, who was in duty bound to champion his own mule. Peg-Leg was far more disgusted than Phip, and grew melancholy as he reflected on the unfairness of our methods. After being jeered and laughed at a few moments, he started off for the bottoms in a sulk to have a hunt all his own, with no one to gobble his hard earned glory and meat at the finish.

We proceeded on our way, hoping to find another jack soon, but no jack appeared. Jim's prophecy of the night before fell flat, but still we hoped with the true heroism of the hunter, who should never be discouraged in his search for game. In some respects I consider the hunting field a very good place to test character.

"Do these jack-rabbits think we'll 'unt hall day?" queried Charlie, with his rising inflection. We were silent, as we had our doubts as to the jacks having any thoughts in the matter. We were some ten miles from home when we started a jack at last, and took after him, horse, dog and man. Charlie B—— was in the lead, and the rabbit was going toward the ranch and corrals of one John Mitchner, a new arrival in these parts, from somewhere in the Indian Territory. The rabbit made straight for a corral and shot through a wire fence, the dog with a graceful bound went over, and the blue mare seemed to be going through, though Charlie succeeded in stopping her, thus saving himself a good scraping. We lost the rabbit, as it got under a hay-rick and Peg was not about to help us out of our difficulty, he having left in a tiff.

Old John came out of his house smoking a corn-cob pipe, and extended his compliments with a graceful "how-de, boys."

"Hello, John! come out and hunt rabbits; you have nothing else to do," was the reply.

"Well I reckon as how I'm gettin' too ole to be chasing them nasty little rabbits over these yar prairies, but this yar a runnin' of horses kinder gets me. If I only had that cow-skin horse now what I used ter own back in old Missouri, I'd show—"

"Oh, come off, John; that old cow-skin business is played out," broke in Jim, who had heard old John discourse on the cow-skin racer until he was sick of it. "You will get the world to moving backwards if you keep dinging away about that old hoss. Why, I met a chap from Missouri the other day what allowed as he knew the cow-skin hoss, and he says he's beat him with a mule once back thar in Missouri," went on Jim.

We realized that Jim had evolved this last fabrication on the spot, with no basis of truth, but were content to see old John's cow-skin ghost of discussion annihilated at once.

Old John removed his pipe, his eyes glistened and he replied vehemently, pointing a long, bony finger at Jim—"That feller's a liar, do ye understan'? That feller's a d——— liar, and it's old John Mitchner as will fill his lyin' hide full of holes ef ye'll jest show him up, do ye understan'? fer I don't allow no Missouri liar to come browsin' about these parts a sayin' as how the cow-skin hoss was ever beat by any critter as wears har—do ye understan', Mr. Jim C———?"

"Oh, yes; I understan', Uncle John. I thought he was a liar at the time, but I did not tell him so, 'cause he had red eyes and was loaded with guns," replied Jim in a conciliatory manner.

"I don't care a peg if he were a man-of-war; you jest allow as I say. I'll make a mineral lead of his carcass if I get a sight on him," added Uncle John, as he grew more resigned, seeming to think the cow-skin stories vindicated by this reckless harangue. "Come, dismount and come in; it's near time fer dinner," said John, as he walked back to the house.

We tied our horses to the fence and followed. "I tell you, boys, if that cow-skin horse ever existed a better horse could have broke old John pretty bad. We'll have to put up a job on old John's sporting blood to-day. You go in, Jim, and run a bluff on him," said Bill to us in a whisper, as we stepped into John's cabin.

We sat about and smoked while old John's boy got a dinner of bacon and eggs. The conversation turned on horses, and with old John in the company, horse talk was a synonym for cow-skin horse talk. At last Jim spoke up, "Say, Uncle John, I don't think you ever owned but one good horse in your life. You hain't any horse in yer corral as could beat a Mexican sheep fer a quarter."

Old John gazed at the stove for a few moments, and then awoke and began: "Wall, my hoss stock ain't nothin' to brag on now, because I hain't got the money that you fellers down in the creek has got fer to buy 'em with, but I've got a little mare down thar in the corral as I've got a notion ken run some shakes."

"How fast, Uncle John?" queried Jim.

"Well, tol'able fast. I reckon as how she's a smarter horse than is hitched to the fence on the outside of the corral."

"Ha! ha! you don't mean it, Uncle John. Why, my baby Push-Bob or grey Prince would shovel sand into her eyes in great shape at a quarter," provokingly retorted Jim.

"Ye've got a great notion of them 'ar horses of yourn. I'm an old man, and I've got done a racin' of horses, but if your hoss can beat mine you can have the mare," replied John Mitchner, fixedly eyeing Jim.

"It's a go—hoss agin hoss," spoke up Jim, rising, "I'll ride mine and you ride yourn."

"Come on," said John, putting on his hat. We all arose and went out. The boy left the bacon and eggs to burn to a cinder on the cook-stove and followed.

"I'll bet Prince can beat either of you," said Bill, at this stage of the proceedings. "I'll ride him, and we'll all three run, the winner to take both —this yer is going to be a horse race, and it's a good time to see whether Prince or Push-Bob is the better horse."

The offer was accepted, and with this understanding the men began to strip their horses and to remove all their superfluous clothes, for the quarter-races on the plains are all ridden bareback, and nearly naked. We began to get excited, and finally I provoked old John into betting with me. He wagered a fine horse and colt, which he pointed out in the corral with the remark, "agin yer yeller nag," and continuing, "This yar is a horse race, and I'm a bettin' man when I race horses, which is something I hain't done this ten years." At the last moment, as we had the track paced off on the level prairie, Bob bet his mare against four head of cattle, to be picked from John's herd. The Englishman wanted a hand, and staked the blue mare against a three-year-old, said to belong to John Mitchner's boy, and Phip mounted the mule and regarded the proceedings as ominous in the extreme.

"Ye'll get beat sure," he whispered to me; but I sneered, "What, that grey mare beat Push-Bob? Why, Phip, what are you thinking of? She's an old brood mare, and looks as though she had come through in the spring instead of off the grass in the fall."

I was to fire the starting shot with old John's musket, and Charlie and Bob were to judge at the other end along with Mitchner's boy.

The three racers came up to the scratch, Bill and Jim sitting their sleek steeds like centaurs. Old Prince had bristled up and moved with great vim and power. Push-Bob swerved about and stretched his neck on the bit. The boys were bare-footed, with their sleeves rolled up and a hand-kerchief tied around their heads. Old John came prancing out, stripped to the waist, on his mare, which indeed looked more game when mounted than running loose in the corral. The old man's grey, thin locks were blowing loose in the wind, and he worked his horse up to the scratch in a very knowing way. We all regarded the race as a foregone conclusion and had really begun to pity old John's impoverishment, but still there was the interest in the bout between Prince and Push-Bob. This was the first time the victors of the White-water bottoms had met, and was alto-gether the greatest race which the country had seen in years. How the boys from the surrounding ranches would have gathered could they have known it, but it is just as well that they did not; for as I fired the gun and the horses scratched away from the mark, Old John went to the front and stayed there to the end, winning by several lengths, while Prince and Push-Bob ran what was called a dead heat, although there was considerable discussion over it for a long time afterwards. There was my dear little Terra gone to the hands of the spoilsman, and the very thought almost broke my heart, as I loved that mare as I shall never love another animal. I went back to the corral, sat down and began to whittle a stick. It took Bob and Charlie a half an hour to walk the quarter of a mile back to the ranch. Bill and Jim said nothing kept them from flying the country to save their horses but the fact that they had no saddles.

Old John rode up, threw himself from his broncho and drawled out: "Thar now; I've been a layin' fer you fellers ever since I came inter these yar parts and I reckon as how I've sort of got ye. If ye'd had more horses with ye, I'd a had a right smart horse herd arter this race"; and then turning to Jim he added, "Mr. Jim, ye're a pretty smart feller, don't ye? P'raps ye'l hev more faith in the cow-skin horse stories now, seein' as how this yar grey mare is known back in parts of Missouri as the cow-skin horse, all along of a circumstance the particulars of which I allow p'raps yer don't keer to hear now," whereat he turned his mare into the corral, went and untied Terra-Cotta, the black mare, the brown horse and the blue mare, which he also turned loose in his horse corral along with a half-dozen herd of his own stock.

"Mr. Jim, will yer be so good as to jest turn that alleged race-horse inter this yar corral, seein' as yer don't own him no more?"

Mr. Jim and Mr. Bill, as old John insisted on calling them in his chilling discourse, did as requested, whereat old John invited us to dinner

OLD JOHN WENT TO THE FRONT AND STAYED THERE TO THE END

and turned on his heel. But no one manifested a disposition to dine. We stood leaning over the corral fence, regarding intently the cow-skin horse, and wondering at the deceitfulness of appearances. Some one suggested that it was a right good distance home but the walking was good.

"Let's borrow the 'osses," suggested the Englishman.

"I'd walk from here to old Mexico before I'd ask old John fer a horse," replied Bill, and we all declined to solicit John's charity in the matter. So the walk began, and a long, solemn tramp it was over the dry plain. Phip rode the mule, as he was a rather old man and not in shape to walk an odd ten miles, and carried the saddles, and the rest of us trudged along beside.

As we neared home, or Bob's ranch, we began to feel gaunt, and Phip cheered us by assurances of some tid-bits in the shape of a can of white pears and a cold goose which Jim had shot some days previous. As we descended into the bottoms, Peg-Leg greeted us, and as he gazed at our solemn procession, it seemed I could detect a smile of comfort on his canine countenance. The boys on the ranch regarded us curiously and seriously, but it gradually dawned upon them, after numerous questions and evasive answers, what had happened, and they retired to the barn, where I thought I heard discordant sounds for an hour after. Phip set up the can of pears and we picked the goose clean from a sense of duty.

"Every man in this country will know of this inside of two days," regretfully sighed Bob.

"If there war any brush hereabouts I'd take to it," asserted Bill, "but there ain't, and we'll have to go down to Hoyt's grocery to-morrow and face the music—and say, gentlemen, it will be pizen."

Phip was dying to work the "I told you so" business, but he was suppressed by ominous threats of dire resort.

We procured horses of Bob and saddled up to go our various ways. As we started, Jim said—

"Well, boys, how do you like running jacks?"

We all laughed and parted as good-humoredly as the circumstances would allow.

That night, Bill and I rode down to Hoyt's grocery and post-office to purchase some necessities, but through the window in the light of the store we could see old John Mitchner perched on a barrel of sugar and a crowd of the boys around him all convulsed with laughter.

"Bill, let's go home," I remarked, and we trotted off up the road into the darkness. ■ ■

A Peccary Hunt in Northern Mexico

The second of Remington's stories, "A Peccary Hunt in Northern Mexico," was published in *Harper's Weekly*, December 1, 1889.

HAVING BEEN AN ARDENT SPORTSMAN all my life, I was greatly interested in the accounts of the peculiar delights of the pursuit of the peccary, as narrated by a mining engineer of my acquaintance, as we sat conversing in the court of an adobe hotel situated in the Mexican town of Hermosillo, State of Sonora. Upon my expressing a desire to participate in an affair of the sort, my friend invited me to go out into the country and try it with him, a suggestion of which I quickly availed myself. As the train on the Sonora Railroad was about leaving for the north, we drove to the depot and boarded it. We traveled some hours, and then alighted at a station with an unpronounceable name. The Sonora River flows through the country in which we were, on its long journey from the Sierra Madre range to the Gulf of California, with small promise of ever reaching its destination, one would think, for the looks of the hot and thirsty sands through which it found its way. The whole aspect of nature was cruel, with its yellow sparkling sands dotted with cactus, chaparral and other thorny growths, which cut and scratch if you are not wary. No agriculture can be practiced except along the river bottoms, in such places as it is possible to conduct water over the land by ditches or acequias. Around this little lonesome depot, squatted away out there

43

in the desert, was a group of people hanging about to see the train come in and go out. They were very swarthy of skin, and dressed in white, and no doubt had knives under their tunics.

My friend the engineer walked up to an old Mexican who was seated on a box in the shade of the station and shook his hand. I was called up and introduced to Senor Samanego. I could make but poor progress with the Spanish conversation, only comprehending the commonest words and phrases. The old fellow was very polite and dignified, as are all Mexican men, and after the engineer had told him that we had come out to hunt peccaries, he was much amused, and chuckled, and passed some words to two slouch-hatted, cotton shirted vaqueros who stood near gazing stupidly at the Gringos, which is the slang name they apply to the Americans, whereat they mounted their ponies and galloped off through the chaparral in a cloud of dust. After a while they returned, leading two saddle ponies, and the old Mexican motioned us to mount them. My mount was a little drooping, demure beast with fleshless limbs, and a huge saddle with tapaderas on the stirrup which nearly swished on the ground. We rode off again under the guidance of Samanego, followed by the two vaqueros. It was nearing sunset, and was growing cooler as we rode. One could not see far, as the chaparral thickets interposed, but wound and worried through them, stirring up a cloud of dust, until we came to an open space, where we could see the adobe walls of Samanego's rancho. Here we dismounted, and I busied myself with making a sketch of the surrounding objects, which were all so strange to an American like myself. The engineer called loudly to me from a stake-fence corral to come down there, which I did, and to my astonishment he pointed to a small animal which was tied with a rope by one hind leg to a post. "There is a peccary for you, natural as life and twice as ugly," said the engineer, laughing. I gazed at the little beast, for he was typical of what I had come to hunt. A small razor-back hog from Arkansas would not be very unlike him, only he was covered with gray hair, and had three-toed feet, more like a dog than a pig. His eyes were set in a very malevolent fashion as he considered the situation, and his whole aspect was one of belligerency, as much as to say, "If only I could get at you I should take a huge piece out of your leg." They say these peccaries are domesticated at times, but for my part I do not think the game would be worth the candle.

I was aroused early next morning, and found myself in the saddle before I was hardly awake. Again we followed the old Mexican, Samanego, off into the great plain, winding about in the chaparral. We followed down the course of a little stream which was fringed with cotton-wood and palm trees. The engineer said that one of the vaqueros had found peccaries the day before, somewhere below, while he was out looking for stray horses. I will here explain that the method for hunting peccaries, as followed by the Mexican vaqueros or cowboys, is peculiar to them, and consists in roping them by adroitly casting their raeta about their body, much in the same way as they do a steer. In this way they are often taken alive. I had learned to throw a rope in an indifferent fashion during my life on the cattle ranges of the north, and concluded to try my hand with it, instead of using a rifle or six-shooter, as the engineer proposed to do. I felt that the life-long skill of the vaqueros would make my un-practiced efforts contemptuous in comparison; but what of that? The sun came up suddenly from behind the blue line of the far off Sierras, and the terrific glare of another day was to begin. The senor called a halt, and after directing his men to do certain things, they trotted off into the brush and were lost to sight. I understood that they were to make a detour and strike the creek some distance below, and there beat up the bush toward our position, thus drawing out any peccaries which might be concealed there. We sat down and rolled and smoked cigarettes in a true spirit of appreciation of our Mexican surroundings, for in Mexico every-one smokes cigarettes. The senor explained that the peccary cannot run as fast as a horse, which statement I did not doubt, as I never saw any animal that could. He also added that the little ponies had been trained to run in the chaparral, and could dodge about so quickly to avoid it that an unskilled rider might suddenly find himself on his back in the sand. He further explained that the peccary had a very short and bad temper, and that he was liable to turn the tables arbitrarily at any moment and transform the scene into peccaries hunting a man.

With these instructions, I began to coil my rope, adjust my six-shooter and to tighten my saddle cinchas and girths. We stood at our horses' heads as the old senor looked up at the sun and said it was time the men got back to us. Presently we heard a rustling in some canebrakes down the creek, followed by quick grunts. "Viniendo, senors," whispered Samanego, as he swung himself into his saddle, and looked sharply at his rope. We also mounted, and as I was fairly seated, the patter of the Mexican ponies came to my ears, and amid a cloud of dust I could see the circling reata and the flying hoofs. I also distinguished a little black form scurrying along in front. Circle, circle, circle flowed the long noose of the rope about the cloud of dust, and with a long-drawn sweep it flew forward in graceful coils and settled about the peccary. The pony quickly swerved, the rope straightened, the pony plunged two or three times and made toward us at top speed, dragging the black object behind. "Quando yo salo el dia, estaba mio frio," yelled the Mexican, in great glee, which was a translation of a bit of American slang made by the engineer the night before, and taken up by the Mexican in his high spirits. He jerked the little pig about like a football, raising such a cloud of dust around his

A PECCARY HUNT IN NORTHERN MEXICO

ears that I had no doubt the little animal would soon want for breath. After this had gone on for a time, and we had admired the graceful horsemanship of the Mexican, the peccary lay still and the Mexican approached him, slowly winding in his rope. He suddenly drew his revolver and shot the prostrate animal. He told the engineer that the beast was shamming death and he shot him for fear he might come to life and make it dangerous for him.

He leaned from his saddle and undid his rope from about the body of the game, again coiled it, and started off at a gallop down the creek. We followed, and could presently hear the cries of the vaqueros, the clatter of the horses' hoofs and could see a cloud of dust coming toward us. One peccary broke cover right in front of us, and then another, until I counted eight. They did not see us until we were nearly onto them, so intent were they on the men behind, and then they swerved. We spurred our horses, and then commenced a mad gallop, with the dust flying and the men yelling. I swung my rope, and aimed to catch a big fellow scurrying along just ahead, when crash I went into a mass of mesquite boughs, which took my hat off and nearly unseated me; but my little pony was in for the hunt, and went along all right, following like a greyhound. The peccaries kept in a bunch, and the old senor was at my side, with the others racing along behind and about us. The senor howled Spanish at me, which I did not understand, but I could see that he was encouraging me to make a cast. I saw my opportunity presently and threw the rope. It settled about my game, but I could not turn my horse as the old Mexican was on my left and I was thus unable to tighten the noose. The peccary, not liking the feeling of the rope in which he was entangling himself at every jump, stopped, and I dashed over him, and just what happened in the dust and confusion that followed I did not keep a strict account of, but I pulled in my pony, dropped my rope, and drew a six-shooter and shot away at the peccary, which was struggling in the sand with the reata more hopelessly entwined about him. The dust settled and I found I had killed a peccary sure enough. The old senor came up shortly and saw my good luck. He dismounted, drew a knife and commenced to skin and cut up the animal on the spot. One of the men was dispatched to where the other dead peccary was, to perform a similar office. These were the only two which we got that day. The old Mexican could easily have gotten another, but he generously gave up his opportunity to me, for which I thanked him. Thus ended a bit of sport which I enjoyed hugely and which I think was quite beyond ordinary methods of hunting. ■■

Antoine's Moose-Yard

During the early 1890's a series of stories appeared in Harper's *New Monthly Magazine*, all written by Julian Ralph. Many of these were illustrated by Remington. Eventually, these stories appeared in book form entitled *On Canada's Frontier*, Harper & Brothers, New York, 1892. This story, "Antoine's Moose-Yard" appeared in Harper's *New Monthly Magazine*, October, 1890. It is included in this book because Remington is a principal character in the piece.

IT WAS THE NIGHT of a great dinner at the club. Whenever the door of the banqueting hall was opened, a burst of laughter or of applause disturbed the quiet talk of a few men who had gathered in the reading-room—men of the sort that extract the best enjoyment from a club by escaping its functions, or attending them only to draw to one side its choicest spirits for never-to-be-forgotten talks before an open fire, and over wine and cigars used sparingly.

"I'm tired," an artist was saying—"so tired that I have a horror of my studio. My wife understands my condition, and bids me go away and rest."

"That is astonishing," said I; "for, as a rule, neither women nor men can comprehend the fatigue that seizes an artist or writer. At most of our homes there comes to be a reluctant recognition of the fact that we say we are tired, and that we persist in the assumption by knocking off work. But human fatigue is measured by the mile of walking, or the cords of firewood that have been cut, and the world will always hold that if we have not hewn wood or tramped all day, it is absurd for us to talk of feeling tired. We cannot alter this; we are too few."

"Yes," said another of the little party. "The world shares the feeling of the Irishman who saw a very large, stout man at work at reporting in a court-room. 'Faith!' said he, 'will ye look at the size of that man—to be airning his living wid a little pincil?' The world would acknowledge our right to feel tired if we used crow-bars to write or draw with; but pencils! pshaw! a hundred weigh less than a pound."

"Well," said I, "all the same, I am so tired that my head feels like cork; so tired that for two days I have not been able to summon an idea or turn a sentence neatly. I have been sitting at my desk writing wretched stuff and tearing it up, or staring blankly out of the window."

"Glorious!" said the artist, startling us all with his vehemence and inapt exclamation. "Why, it is providential that I came here to-night. If that's the way you feel, we are a pair, and you will go with me and rest. Do you hunt? Are you fond of it?"

"I know all about it," said I, "but I have not definitely determined whether I am fond of it or not. I have been hunting only once. It was years ago, when I was a mere boy. I went after deer with a poet, an editor, and a railroad conductor. We journeyed to a lovely valley in Mifflin County, Pennsylvania, and put ourselves in the hands of a man seven feet high, who had a flintlock musket a foot taller than himself, and a wife who gave us saleratus bread and a bowl of pork fat for supper and breakfast. We were not there at dinner. The man stationed us a mile apart on what he said were the paths, or "runways," the deer would take. Then he went to stir the game up with his dogs. There he left us from sunrise till supper, or would have left us had we not with great difficulty found one another, and enjoyed the exquisite woodland quiet and light and shade together, mainly flat on our backs, with the white sails of the sky floating in an azure sea above the reaching fingers of the tree-tops. The editor marred the occasion with an unworthy suspicion that our hunter was at the village tavern picturing to his cronies what simple donkeys we were, standing a mile apart in the forsaken woods. But the poet said something so pregnant with philosophy that it always comes back to me with the mention of hunting. 'Where is your gun?' he was asked, when we came upon him, pacing the forest path, hands in pockets, and no weapon in sight. 'Oh, my gun?' he repeated. 'I don't know. Somewhere in among the trees. I covered it with leaves so as not to see it. After this, if I go hunting again, I shall not take a gun. It is very cold and heavy, and more or less dangerous in the bargain. You never use it, you know. I go hunting every few years, but I never yet have had to fire my gun, and I begin to see that it is only brought along in deference to a tradition descending from an era when men got something more than fresh air and scenery on a hunting trip.'"

The other laughed at my story, but the artist regarded me with an expression of pity. He is a famous hunter—a genuine, devoted hunter—and one might almost as safely speak a light word of his relations as of his favorite mode of recreation.

"Fresh air!" said he; "scenery! Humph! Your poet would not know which end of a gun to aim with. I see that you know nothing at all about hunting, but I will pay you the high compliment of saying that I can make a hunter of you. I have always insisted heretofore that a hunter must begin in boyhood; but never mind, I'll make a hunter of you at thirty-six. We will start to-morrow morning for Montreal, and in twenty-four hours you shall be in the greatest sporting region in America, incomparably the greatest hunting district. It is great because Americans do not know of it, and because it has all of British America to keep it supplied with game. Think of it! In twenty-four hours we shall be tracking moose near Hudson Bay, for Hudson Bay is not much farther from New York than Chicago —another fact that few persons are aware of."

Environment is a positive force. We could feel that we were disturbing what the artist would call "the local tone," by rushing through the city's streets next morning with our guns slung upon our backs. It was just at the hour when the factory hands and the shop-girls were out in force, and the juxtaposition of those elements of society with two portly men bearing guns created a positive sensation. In the cars the artist held forth upon the terrors of the life upon which I was about to venture. He left upon my mind a blurred impression of sleeping out-of-doors, like human cocoons, done up in blankets, while the savage mercury lurked in unknown depths below the zero mark. He said the camp fire would have to be fed every two hours of each night, and he added, without contradiction from me, that he supposed he would have to perform this duty as he was accustomed to it. Lest his forecast should raise my anticipation of pleasure extravagantly, he added that those hunters were fortunate who had fires to feed; for his part he had once walked around a tree stump a whole night to keep from freezing. He supposed that we would perform our main journeying on snow-shoes, but how we should enjoy that he could not say, as his knowledge of snow-shoeing was limited.

At this point the inevitable offspring of fate, who is always at a traveller's elbow with a fund of alarming information, cleared his throat as he sat opposite us, and inquired whether he had overheard that we did not know much about snow-shoes. An interesting fact concerning them, he said, was that they seemed easy to walk with at first, but if the learner fell down with them on, it usually needed a considerable portion of a tribe of Indians to put him back on his feet. Beginners only fell down, however, in attempting to cross a log or stump, but the forest where we were going was literally floored with such obstructions. The first day's effort to navigate with snow-shoes, he remarked, is usually accompanied by a terrible malady called mal de raquette, in which the cords of one's legs become knotted in great and excruciatingly painful bunches. The cure for this is to "walk it off the next day, when the agony is yet more intense than at first." As the stranger had reached his destination, he had little more than time to remark that the moose is an exceedingly vicious animal, invariably attacking all hunters who fail to kill him with the first shot. As the stranger stepped upon the car platform he let fall a simple but touching eulogy upon a dear friend who had recently lost his life by being literally cut in two, lengthwise, by a moose who struck him on the chest with its rigidly stiffened forelegs. The artist protested that the stranger was a sensationalist, unsupported by either the camp-fire gossip or the literature of hunters. Yet one man that night found his slumber tangled with what the garrulous alarmist had been saying.

In Montreal one may buy clothing not to be had in the United States: woolens thick as boards, hosiery that wards off the cold as armour resists missiles, gloves as heavy as shoes, yet soft as kid, fur caps and coats at prices and in a variety that interest poor and rich alike, blanket suits that are more picturesque than any other masculine garment worn north of the city of Mexico, tuques, and moccasins, and, indeed, so many sorts of clothing we Yankees know very little of that at a glance we say the Montrealers are foreigners. Montreal is the gayest city on this continent, and I have often thought that the clothing there is largely responsible for that condition.

A New Yorker disembarking in Montreal in midwinter finds the place inhospitably cold, and wonders how, as well as why, any one lives there. I well remember standing years ago beside a toboggan slide, with my teeth chattering, and my very marrow slowly congealing, when my attention was called to the fact that a dozen ruddy-cheeked, bright-eyed, laughing girls were grouped in snow that reached their knees. I asked a Canadian lady how that could be possible, and she answered with a list of the principal garments those girls were wearing.

Mr. W. C. Van Horne, the President of the Canadian Pacific Railroad, proved a friend in need. He dictated a few telegrams that agitated the people of a vast section of country between Ottawa and the great lakes. And in the afternoon the answers came flying back. These were from various points where Hudson Bay posts are situated. At one or two the Indian trappers and hunters were all away on their winter expeditions; from another a famous white hunter had just departed with a party of gentlemen. At Mattawa, in Ontario, moose were close at hand and plentiful, and two skilled Indian hunters were just in from a trapping expedition; but the post factor, Mr. Rankin, was sick in bed, and the Indians were on a spree. To Mattawa we decided to go. It was a twelve hour journey from New York to Montreal, and an eleven-hour journey from Montreal to the heart of this hunter's paradise; so that, had we known at just which point to enter the forest, we could have taken the trail in twenty-four hours from the metropolis, as the artist had predicted.

Our first taste of the frontier, at Peter O'Farrall's Ottawa Hotel, in Mattawa, was delicious in the extreme. O'Farrall used to be game-keeper to the Marquis of Waterford, and thus got "a taste of the quality" that prompted him to assume the position he has chosen as the most lordly hotel-keeper in Canada. We do not know what sort of men own our great New York and Chicago and San Francisco hotels, but certainly they cannot lead more leisurely, complacent lives than Mr. O'Farrall. He has a bar-tender to look after male visitors and the bar, and a matronly relative to see to the women and the kitchen, so that the land-lord arises when he likes to enjoy each succeeding day of ease and prosperity. He has been known to exert himself, as when he chased a man who spoke slighteningly of his liquor. And he was momentarily ruffled at the trying conduct of the artist on this hunting trip. The artist could not find his overcoat, and had the temerity to refer the matter to Mr. O'Farrall.

"Sir," said the artist, "what do you suppose has become of my over-coat? I cannot find it anywhere."

"I don't know anything about your botheration overcoat," said Mr. O'Farrall. "Sure, I've trouble enough kaping thrack of me own."

The reader may be sure that O'Farrall was rightly recommended to us, and that it is a well managed and popular place, with good beds and excellent fare, and with no extra charge for the delightful addition of the host himself, who is very tall and dignified and humorous, and who is the oddest and yet most picturesque-looking public character in the Dominion. Such an oddity is certain to attract queer characters to his side, and Mr. O'Farrall is no exception to the rule. One of the waiter-girls in the dining-room was found never by any chance to know anything that she was asked about. For instance, she had never heard of Mr. Rankin, the chief man of the place. To every question she made answer, "Sure, there does be a great dale goin' on here and I know nothin' of it." Of her the artist ventured the theory that "she could not know everything on a waiter-girl's salary." John, the bar-tender, was a delightful study. No matter what a visitor laid down in the smoking-room, John picked it up and carried it behind the bar. Everyone was continually losing something and searching for it, always to observe that John was able to produce it with a smile and the wise remark that he had taken the lost article and put it away "for fear someone would pick it up." Finally, there was Mr. O'Farrall's dog. A ragged, time-worn, petulant terrier, no bigger than a pintpot. Mr. O'Farrall nevertheless called him "Fairy," and said he kept him "to protect the village children against wild bears."

I shall never be able to think of Mattawa as it is—a plain little lumber town on the Ottawa River, with the wreck and ruin of once grand scenery hemming it in on all sides, in the form of ragged mountains, literally ravaged by fire and the axe. Hints of it come back to me in dismembered bits that prove it to have been interesting; vignettes of little school boys in blanket suits and moccasins, of great spirited horses forever racing ahead of fur-laden sleighs, and of troops of olive-skinned French Canadian girls, bundled up from their feet to those mischievous features which shot roguish glances at the artist—the biggest man, the people said, who had ever been seen in Mattawa. But the place will ever yield back to my mind the impression I got of the wonderful preparations that were made for our adventure—preparations that seemed to busy or to interest nearly everyone in the village. Our Indians had come in from the Indian village three miles away, and had said they had had enough drink. Mr. John DeSousa, accountant at the post, took charge of them and of us, and the work of loading a great portage sleigh went on apace. The men of sporting tastes came out and lounged in front of the post, and gave helpful advice; the Indians and clerks went to and from the sleigh laden with bags of necessaries, the harness-maker made for us belts such as the lumbermen use to preclude the possibility of in-curable strains in the rough life in the wilderness. The help at O'Farrall's assisted in repacking what we needed, so that our trunks and town clothing could be stored. Mr. DeSousa sent messengers hither and thither for es-sentials not in stock at the post. Some women, even, were set at work to make "neaps" for us, a neap being a sort of slipper or unlaced shoe made of heavy blanketing and worn outside one's stockings, to give added warmth to the feet.

"You see, this is no casual rabbit hunt," said the artist. The remark will live in Mattawa many a year.

The Hudson Bay Company's posts differ. In the wilderness they are forts surrounded by stockades, but within the bounderies of civilization they are stores. That at old Fort Garry, now called Winnipeg, is a splendid emporium, rather more like the establishment at Whiteley, "the universal provider" of London, than anything in the United States. That at Mattawa is like a village store in the United States, except that the top story is laden with guns, traps, snow-shoes and the skins of wild beasts; while an outbuilding in the rear is the repository of scores of birch-bark canoes, the carriages of British America. Mr. Rankin, the factor there, lay in a bed of suffering and could not see us. Yet it seemed difficult to believe that we could be made the recipients of greater or more kindly attentions than were lavished upon us by his accountant, Mr. DeSousa. He ordered our tobacco ground for us ready for our pipes; selected the finest from among those extraordinary blankets that have been made exclusively for this company for hundreds of years; picked out the largest snow-shoes in his stock; bade us lay aside the gloves we had brought, and take mittens such as he produced, and for which we thanked him in our hearts many times afterward; planned our outfit of food with the wisdom of an old cam-paigner; bethought himself to send for baker's bread; ordered high legs sewed on our moccasins—in a word, he made it possible for us to say afterward that absolutely nothing had been overlooked or slighted in fitting out our expedition.

As I sat in the sleigh, tucked in under heavy skins and leaning at royal ease against other furs that covered a bale of hay, it seemed to me that I had become part of one of such pictures as we all have seen, portraying historic expeditions in Russia or Siberia. We carried fifteen hundred pounds of traps and provisions for camping, stabling, and food for men and beasts. We were five in all, two hunters, two Indians and a teamster. We set out with the two mettlesome horses ahead, the driver on a high seat formed of a second bale of hay, ourselves lolling back under our furs, and the two Indians striding along over the resonant cold snow behind us. It was beginning to be evident that a great deal of effort and machinery was needed to make "a hunter" of a city man, and that it was going to be done thoroughly—two thoughts of a highly flattering nature.

We were now clad for Arctic weather, and perhaps nothing except a mummy was ever "so dressed up" as we were. We each wore two pairs of the heaviest woolen stockings I ever saw, and over them ribbed bicycle stockings that came to our knees. Over these in turn were our "neaps," and then our moccasins, laced tightly around our ankles. We had on two suits of flannels of extra thickness, flannel shirts, reefing jackets, and "capeaux," as they call their long hooded blanket coats, longer than snow-shoe coats. On our heads we had knitted tuques, and on our hands mittens and gloves. We were bound for Antoine's moose-yard, near Crooked Lake.

The explanation of the term "Moose-yard" made moose hunting appear a simple operation. A moose-yard is the feeding ground of a herd of moose, and our head Indian, Alexandre Antoine, knew where there was one. Each herd or family of these great wild cattle had two such feeding grounds and they are said to go alternately from one to the other, never herding in one two years in succession. In the region of Canada they weigh between six-hundred and twelve-hundred pounds. Whether they desert a yard for twelve months because of the damage they do it in feeding upon the branches and foilage of soft-wood trees and shrubs, or whether it is instinctive caution that directs their movements, no one can more than conjecture.

Their yards are always where soft-woods are plentiful, and water is near, and during a winter they will feed over a region from half a mile to a mile square. The prospect of going directly to the fixed home of a herd of moose almost robbed the trip of that speculative element that gives the greatest zest to hunting. But we knew not what the future held for us. Not even the artist, with all his experience, conjectured what was in store for us. And what was to come came almost immediately.

The journey began upon a good highway, over which we slid as comfortably as any ladies in their carriages, and with the sleigh-bells flinging their cheery music out over a desolate valley, with a leaden river at the bottom, and with small mountains rolling all about. The timber was cut off them, except here and there a few red or white pines that reared their green, brush-like tops against the general blanket of snow. The dull sky hung sullenly above, and now and then a raven flew by, croaking harsh disapproval of our intrusion. To warn us of what we were to expect, Antoine had made a shy Indian joke, one of the few I ever heard. "In small little while," said he, "we come to all sorts of a road. Me call it that 'cause we get every sort riding, then you sure be suited."

At five miles out we came to this remarkable highway. It can no more be adequately described here than could the experiences of a man who goes over Niagara Falls in a barrel. The reader must try to imagine the most primitive sort of a highway conceivable; one that has been made by merely felling trees through a forest in a path wide enough for a team and wagon. All the tree stumps were left in their places, and every here and there were rocks, some no larger than a bale of cotton, and some as small as a bushel basket. To add to the other alluring qualities of the road, there were tree trunks now and then directly across it, and, as a further inducement to traffic, the highway was frequently interrupted by "pitch holes." Some of these would be called pitch holes anywhere. They were at points where a rill crossed the road, or the road crossed the corner of a marsh. But there were other pitch holes that any intelligent New Yorker would call ravines or gullies. These were at points where one hill ran down to the water-level and another immediately arose precipitately, there being a water course between the two. In all such places there was deep black mud and broken ice. However, these were mere features of the character of the road—a character too profound for me to attempt to portray it. When the road was not inclined either straight down or straight up, it coursed along the slanting side of a steep hill, so that a vehicle could keep to it only by falling against the forest at the under side and carroming along from tree to tree.

Such was the road. The manner of traveling it was quite as astounding. For nothing short of what Alphonse, the teamster, did would I destroy a man's character, but Alphonse was the next thing to an idiot. He made that dreadful journey at a gallop! The first time he upset the sleigh and threw me with one leg thigh-deep between a stone and a tree trunk, besides sending the artist flying over my head like a shot from a sling, he reseated himself and remarked: "That makes tree time I upset in dat place. Hi, there! Get up!" It never occurred to him to stop because a giant tree had fallen across the trail. "Look out! Hold tight!" he would call out, and then he would take the obstruction at a jump. The horses were mammoth beasts, in the best fettle, and the sleigh was of the solidest, strongest pattern. There were places where even Alphonse was anxious to drive with caution. Such were the ravines and underbridged waterways. But one of the horses had cut himself badly in such a place a year before, and both now made it a rule to take all such places flying. Fancy the results! The leap in air, and then the crash of the sled as it landed, the snap of the harness chains, the snorts of the winded beasts, the yells of the driver, the anxiety and nervousness of the passengers!

At one point we had an exciting adventure of a far different sort. There was a moderately good stretch of road ahead, and we invited the Indians to jump in and ride awhile. We noticed that they took occasional draughts from a bottle. They finished a full pint, and presently Alexandre produced another and larger vial. Every one knows what a drunken Indian is, and so did we. We ordered the sleigh stopped and all hands out for "a talk." Firmly, but with both power and reason on our side, we demanded a promise that not another drink should be taken, or that the horses be turned toward Mattawa at once. The promise was freely given.

"But what is that stuff? Let me see it," one of the hunters asked.

"It is de 'igh wine," said Alexandre.

"High wine? Alcohol?" exclaimed the hunter, and, impulse being quicker than reason sometimes, flung the bottle high into the air into the bush. It was an injudicious action, but both of us at once prepared to defend and reinforce it, of course. As it happened, the Indians saw that no unkindness or unfairness was intended, and neither sulked or made trouble afterwards.

We were now deep in the bush. Occasionally we passed a "Brule," or tract denuded of trees, and littered with trunks and tops of trunks rejected by the lumbermen. But every mile took us nearer to the undisturbed primeval forest, where the trees shoot up forty feet before the branches begin. There were no houses, teams, or men. In a week in the bush we saw no other sign of civilization than what we brought or made. All around us rose the motionless regiments of the forest, with the snow beneath them, and their branches and twigs printing lacework in the sky. The signs of game were numerous, and varied to an extent that I never heard of before. There were few spaces of the length of twenty-five feet in which the track of some wild beast or bird did not cross the road. The Indians read this writing in the snow, so that the forest was to them as a book would be to us. "What is that?" "And that?" "And that?" I kept inquiring. The answers told me more eloquently than any man can describe it the story of the abundance of game in that easily accessible wilderness. "Dat red deer," Antoine replied. "Him fox." "Dat bear track; dat squirrel; dat rabbit." "Dat moose track; pass las' week." "Dat partridge; dat wolf." Or perhaps it was the trail of a marten, or a beaver, or a weasel, or a fisher, mink, lynx, or otter that he pointed out, for all these "signs" were there, and nearly all were repeated again and again. Of the birds that were plentiful there the principal kinds are partridge, woodcock, crane, geese, duck gull, loon and owl.

When the sun set we prepared to camp, selecting a spot near a tiny rill. The horses were tethered to a tree, with their harness still on, and blankets thrown over them. We cleared a little space by the roadside, using our snow-shoes for shovels. The Indians, with their axes, turned up the moss and leaves, and leveled the small shoots and brushwood. Then one went off to cut balsam boughs for bedding, while the other set up two crotched sticks, with a pole upon them resting in the crotches, and throwing the canvas of an "A" tent over the frame, he looped the bottom of the tent to small pegs, and banked snow lightly all around it. The little aromatic branches of balsam were laid evenly upon the ground, a fur robe was thrown over the leaves, our enormous blankets were spread half open side by side, and two coats were rolled up and thrown down for pillows. Pierre, the second Indian, made tiny slivers of some soft wood, and tried to start a fire. He failed. Then Alexandre Antoine brought two handfuls of bark, and lighting a small piece with a match, proceeded to build a fire in the most painstaking manner, and with an ingenuity that was most interesting. First he made a fire that could have been started in a teacup. Then he built above and around it a skeleton tent of bits of soft wood, six to nine inches in length. This gave him a fire of the dimensions of a high hat. Next, he threw down two great bits of timber, one on either side of the fire, and a still larger back-log, and upon these he heaped split soft wood. While this was being done, Pierre assailed one great tree after another, and brought them crashing down with noises that startled the forest quiet. Alphonse had opened the provision bags, and presently two tin pails filled with water swung from saplings over the fire, and a pan of fat salt pork was frizzling upon the blazing wood. The darkness grew dead black, and the dancing flames peopled the near forest with dodging shadows. Almost in the time it has taken me to write it, we were squatting on our heels around the fire, each with a massive cutting of bread, a slice of fried pork in a tin plate, and half a pint of tea, precisely as hot as molten lead, in a tin cup. Supper was a necessity, not a luxury, and was hurried out of the way accordingly. Then the men built their camp beside ours in front of the fire, and followed that by felling three or four monarchs of the bush. Nothing surprised me so much as the amount of wood consumed in these open-air fires. In five days at our permanent camp we made a great hole in the forest.

But the first night in the open air, abed with nature, with British America as a bedroom! Only I can tell of it, for the others slept. The stillness was intense. There was no wind, and not an animal or bird uttered a cry. The logs cracked and sputtered and popped, the horses shook their chains, the men all snored—white and red alike. The horses pounded the hollow earth; the logs broke and fell upon the cinders; one of the men talked in his sleep. But over and through it all the stillness grew. Then the fire sank low, the cold became intense, the light was lost, and the darkness swallowed everything. Some one got up awkwardly, with muttering, and flung wood upon the red ashes, and presently all that had passed was re-experienced.

The ride next day was more exciting than the first stage. It was like the journey of a gun-carriage across country in a hot retreat. The sled was actually upset only once, but to prevent that happening fifty times the Indians kept springing at the uppermost side of the flying vehicle, and hanging to the side poles to pull the toppling construction down upon both runners. Often we were advised to leap out for safety's sake; at other times we wished we had leaped out. For several hours we were flung about like cotton spools that were being polished in a revolving cylinder. And yet we were obliged to run long distances after the hurtling sleigh—long enough to tire us. The artist, who had spent years in rude scenes among rough men, said nothing at the time. What was the use? But afterward, in New York, he remarked that this was the roughest traveling he had ever experienced.

The signs of game increased. Deer and bear and wolf and fox and moose were evidently numerous around us. Once we stopped, and the Indians became excited. What they had taken for old moose tracks were the week old footprints of a man. It seems strange, but they felt obliged to know what a man had gone into the bush for a week ago. They followed the signs, and came back smiling. He had gone in to cut hemlock boughs; we would find traces of a camp near by. We did. In a country where men are so few, they busy themselves about one another. Four or five days later, while we were hunting, these Indians came to the road and stopped suddenly, as horses do when lassoed. With a glance they read that two teams had passed during the night, going toward our camp. When we re-turned to camp the teams had been there, and our teamster had talked to the drivers. Therefore that load was lifted from the minds of the Indians. But their knowledge of the bush was marvelous. One point in the woods was precisely like another to us, yet the Indians would leap off the sleigh now and then and dive into the forest, to return with a trap hidden there months before, or to find a great iron kettle.

"Do you never get lost?" I asked Alexandre.

"Me get los'? No, no get los'."

"But how do you find your way?"

"Me fin' way easy. Me know way me come, or me follow my tracks, or me know by de sun. If no sun, me look at trees. Trees grow more branches on side toward sun, and got rough bark on north side. At night me know by see de stars."

We camped in a log hut Alexandre had built for a hunting camp. It was very picturesque and substantial, built of huge logs, and caulked with moss.

It had a great earthen bank in the middle for a fireplace, with an equally large opening in the roof, boarded several feet high at the sides to form a chimney. At one corner of the fire bank was an ingenious crane, capable of being raised and lowered, and projecting from a pivoted post, so that the long arm could be swung over or away from the fire. At one end of the single apartment were two roomy bunks built against the wall. With extraordinary skill and quickness the Indians whittled a spade out of a board, performing the task with an axe, an implement they can use as white men use a penknife, an implement they value more highly than a gun. They made a broom of balsam boughs, and dug and swept the dirt off the floor and walls, speedily making the cabin neat and clean. Two new bunks were put up for us, and bedded with balsam boughs and skins. Shelves were already up, and spread with pails and bottles, tin cups and plates, knives and forks, canned goods etc. On them and on the floor were our stores.

We had a week's outfit, and we needed it, because for five days we could not hunt on account of the crust on the snow, which made such a noise when a human foot broke through it that we could not have approached any wild animal within half a mile. On the third day it rained, but without melting the crust. On the fourth day it snowed furiously, burying the crust under two inches of snow. On the fifth day we got our moose.

In the meantime the log cabin was our home. Alexandre and Pierre cut down trees every day for the fire, and Pierre disappeared for hours every now and then to look after traps set for otter, beaver and marten. Alphonse attended his horses and served as cook. He could produce hotter tea than any other man in the world. I took mine for a walk in the arctic cold three times a day, the artist learned to pour from his one cup to another with amazing dexterity, and the Indians lifted their pans and threw the liquid fire down throats that had been inured to high wines. Whenever the fire was low, the cold was intense. Whenever it was heaped with logs, all the heat flew directly through the roof, and spiral blasts of cold air were sucked through every crack between logs in the cabin walls. Whenever the door opened, the cabin filled with smoke. Smoke clung to all we ate or wore. At night the fire kept burning out, and we arose with chattering teeth to build it anew. The Indians were then to be seen with their blankets pushed down to their knees, asleep in their shirts and trousers. At mealtimes we had bacon or pork, speckled or lake trout, bread and butter, stewed tomatoes, and tea. There were two stools for the five men, but they only complicated the discomfort of those who got them; for it was found that if we put our tin plates on our knees, they fell off; if we held them in our hand, we could not cut the pork and hold the bread with the other hand; while if we put the plates on the floor beside the tea, we could not reach them. In a month we might have solved the problem. Life in that log shanty was precisely the life of the early settlers of this country. It was bound to produce great characters or early death. There could be no middle course with such an existence.

Partridge fed in the brush impudently before us. Rabbits bobbed about in the clearing before the door. Squirrels sat upon the logs near by and gourmandized and chattered. Great saucy birds, like mouse-colored robins, and called mid-birds, stole our provender if we left it out-of-doors half an hour, and one day we saw a red deer jump in the bush a hundred yards away. Yet we got no game, because we knew there was a moose-yard within two miles on one side and within three miles on the other, and we dared not shoot our rifles lest we frighten the moose. Moose were all we were after. There was a lake near by, and the trout in those lakes up there attain remarkable size and numbers. We heard of thirty-five pound speckled trout, of lake trout twice as large, and of enormous muskallonge. The most reliable persons told of lakes farther in the wilderness where the trout are thick as salmon in the British Columbia streams, so thick as to seem to fill the water. We were near a lake that was supposed to have been fished out by lumbermen a year before, yet it was no sport at all to fish there. With a short stick and two yards of line and a bass hook baited with pork we brought up four-pound and five-pound beauties faster than we wanted them for food. Truly we were in a splendid hunting country, like the Adirondacks eighty years ago, but thousands of times as extensive.

Finally we started for moose. Our Indians asked if they might take their guns. We gave the permission. Alexandre, a thin wiry man of forty years, carried an old Henry rifle in a woolen case open at one end like a stocking. He wore a short blanket coat and tuque, and trousers tied tight below the knee, and let into his moccasin-tops. He and his brother Francois are famous Hudson Bay Company trappers and are two-thirds Algonquin and one-third French. He has a typical swarthy angular Indian face and a French mustache and goatee. Naturally, if not by rank, a leader among his men, his manner is commanding and his appearance grave. He talks bad French fluently, and makes wretched headway in English. Pierre is a short, thick-set, walnut-stained man of thirty-five, almost pure Indian, and almost a perfect specimen of physical development. He seldom spoke while on this trip, but he impressed us with his strength, endurance, quickness, and knowledge of woodcraft. Poor fellow! he had only a shot-gun, which he loaded with buckshot. It had no case, and both men carried their pieces grasped by the barrels and shouldered, with the butts behind them.

We set out in Indian-file, plunging at once into the bush. Never was forest scenery more exquisitely beautiful than on that morning as the day broke, for we breakfasted at four o'clock, and started immediately afterwards. Everywhere the view was fairy-like. There was not snow enough for snow-shoeing. But the fresh fall of snow was immaculately white, and flecked the scene apparently from earth to sky, for there was not a branch, or twig, or limb or spray of evergreen, or wart or fungus growth upon any tree, that did not bear its separate burden of snow. It was a bridal dress, not a winding-sheet, that Dame Nature was trying on that morning. And in the bright fresh green of the firs and pines we saw her complexion peeping out above her spotless gown, as one sees the rosy cheeks or black eyes of a girl wrapped in ermine.

Mile after mile we walked, up mountain and down dale, slapped in the face by twigs, knocking snow down the back of our necks, slipping knee-deep in bog mud, tumbling over loose stones, climbing across interlaced logs, dropping to the height of one thigh between tree trunks, sliding, falling, tight-rope walking on branches over thin ice, but forever following the cat-like tread of Alexandre with his seven-league stride and long winded persistence. Suddenly we came to a queer sort of clearing dotted with protuberances like the bubbles on molasses beginning to boil. It was a beaver meadow. The bumps in the snow covered stumps of trees the beavers had gnawed down. The Indians were looking at some trough-like tracks in the snow, like the trail of a tired man who had dragged his heels. "Moose; going this way," said Alexandre; and we turned and walked in the tracks. Across the meadow and across a lake and up another mountain they led us. Then we came upon fresher prints. At each new track the Indians stooped, and making a scoop of one hand, brushed the new-fallen snow lightly out of the indentations. Thus they read the time at which the print was made. "Las' week," "Day 'fore yesterday," they whispered. Presently they bent over again, the light snow flew, and one whispered, "This morning."

Stealthily Alexandre swept ahead; carefully we followed. We dared not break a twig, or speak, or slip, or stumble. As it was, the breaking of the crust was still far too audible. We followed a little stream, and approached a thick growth of tamarack. We had no means of knowing that a herd of moose was lying in that thicket, resting after feeding. We knew it afterward. Alexandre motioned to us to get our guns ready. We each threw a cartridge from the cylinder into the barrel, making a "click, click" that was abominably loud. Alexandre forged ahead. In five minutes we heard him call aloud: "Moose gone. We los' him." We hastened to his side. He pointed at some tracks in which the prints were closer together than any we had seen.

"See, he trot," Alexandre explained.

In another five minutes we had all but completed a circle, and were on the other side of the tamarack thicket. And there were the prints of the bodies of the great beasts. We could see even the imprint of the hair of their coats. All around were broken twigs and balsam needles. The moose had left the branches ragged, and on every hand the young bark was chewed or rubbed raw. Loading our rifles had lost us a herd of moose.

Back once again at the beaver dam, Alexandre and Pierre studied the moose-tramped snow and talked earnestly. They agreed that a desperate battle had been fought there between two bull moose a week before, and that those bulls were not in the "Yard" where we had blundered. They examined the tracks over an acre or more, and then strode off at an obtuse angle from our former trail. Pierre, apparently not satisfied, kept dropping behind or disappearing in the bush at one side of us. So magnificent was his skill at his work that I missed him at times, and at other times found him putting his feet down where mine were lifted up without ever hearing a sound of his step or of his contact with the undergrowth. Alexandre presently motioned us with a warning gesture. He slowed his pace to short steps, with long pauses between. He saw everything that moved, heard every sound; only a deer could throw more and keener faculties into play than this born hunter. He heard a twig snap. We heard nothing. Pierre was away on a side search. Alexandre motioned us to be ready. We crept close together, and I scarcely breathed. We moved cautiously, a step at a time, like chessmen. It was impossible to get an unobstructed view a hundred feet ahead, so thick was the soft-wood growth. It seemed out of the question to try to shoot at that distance. We were descending a hillside into marshy ground. We crossed a corner of a grove of young alders, and saw before us a gentle slope thickly grown with evergreen—tamarack the artist called it. Suddenly Alexandre bent forward and raised his gun. Two steps forward gave us his view. Five moose were fifty yards away, alarmed and ready to run. A big bull in the front of the group had already thrown back his antlers. By impulse rather than through reason I took aim at a second bull. He was half a height lower down the slope, and to be seen through a web of thin foliage. Alexandre and the artist fired as with a single pull at one trigger. The foremost bull staggered and fell forward, as if his knees had been broken. He was hit twice—in the heart and in the neck. The second bull and two cows and a calf plunged into the bush and disappeared. Pierre found the bull a mile away, shot through the lungs.

It had taken us a week to kill our moose in a country where they were common game. That was "Hunter's luck" with a vengeance. But at another season such a delay could scarcely occur. The time to visit that district is in the autumn, before snow falls. Then in a week one ought to be able to bag a moose, and move into the region, farther west and north of the great lakes, where caribou are plenty. ■ ■

In Harper's *New Monthly Magazine* there appeared two of Remington's stories based on canoeing. The first to be published was "Black Water and Shallows" which appeared in the August, 1893 issue and was later published in Remington's famous book, *Pony Tracks*. This story narrates the events of a trip he made down the Oswegatchie River in 1893 accompanied by one of his two favorite Adirondack guides, Harrison "Has" Rasbeck. This river has its beginning in the heart of the Adirondack Mountains, flows into Cranberry Lake, which is also a locale in the story, and takes up its course again in a never ending series of turns and eventually empties into the St. Lawrence River.

The second of the two stories is entitled "The Strange Days That Came To Jimmy Friday" which made its appearance in the same magazine in August, 1896 and later became part of the book by Remington titled *Crooked Trails*. This story appears later in the book.

It is small wonder that these stories were written. The artist loved canoeing passionately. It gave him an outlet for his boundless energy, his love for the out-of-doors, the thrill of the uncertain and

the unexpected. It stimulated his mental power and keyed his sense
of observation. It provided him a wholesome communion with
nature.

It is doubtful if there was any place on earth, excepting his
beloved west, that Remington loved so dearly as his own St. Lawrence country and the Canadian Provinces beyond. His many trips
to this land of the north, his repeated references to it, his knowledge
of its ways attest to this. As an ardent canoeing enthusiast he knew
of no place within reasonable limits where the sport could be so
thoroughly enjoyed and rewarding.

" 'Best place on earth; feel my arm.' No rowboat for him. It
is as tame as riding a broken bronco, as for sailing a boat, he would
'just as soon ride a street car.' "[6]

On his little island kingdom of Inglenook[7] he and his canoe
were inseparable.

At sunset his favorite diversion was to paddle out upon the river
and watch the changing tints of the sky and the water.

" 'Seems as if I must paint them—seems as if they would never
be so beautiful again.' "[8]

"One evening, when the gleam of the full moon drove a path
of sparkling silver from shore to shore, and the stars danced an

FREDERIC REMINGTON IN HIS CANOE: "BEST EXERCISE ON EARTH," HE SAYS.

FREDERIC REMINGTON AND HIS CANOE

accompanyment on the polished expanse of blue, Remington came over from Inglenook. He was bent upon a paddle up the river.

" 'Come along,' he said to a friend watching the view from my veranda. 'This is no place to enjoy such a picture. You want to get away from everything civilized to catch the spirit of this thing—away from the house and people's gabble.'

"Just after sunrise, a day before he was to close up his island home for the summer and return to the city, he paddled out to the little bay in back of his island and painted a sketch of his boathouse, the white rocks and green pines that lined the shore.

" 'First time I've touched the brush this summer,' said he. 'Got to take some of the light and water home with me to look at this winter. Just live to come up here—can't beat it anywhere—'cept out on the plains.' "[9]

[6] Edwin Wildman, "Frederic Remington, the Man," *Outing* Magazine, March, 1903.

[7] In an excellent little pamphlet entitled "Frederic Remington In The Land Of His Youth" prepared for Canton's Remington Centennial Observance—1961, Mr. Atwood advises that in 1898 Remington had paid a Mr. George Shephard $6,000 for a five-acre island, Inglenook, of the Cedar Island group in Chippewa Bay on the St. Lawrence.

[8] Wildman, *op. cit.*

[9] Wildmann, *op. cit.*

BLACK WATER

HUNG UP

Black Water and Shallows

THE MORNING BROKE GRAY and lowering, and the clouds rolled in heavy masses across the sky. I was sitting out on a log washing a shirt, and not distinguishing myself as a laundryman either, for one shirt will become excessively dirty in a week, and no canoeist can have more than that, as will be seen when you consider that he has to carry everything which he owns on his back. My guide had packed up our little "kit" and deposited it skillfully in the Necoochee—a sixteen-foot canoe of the Rice Lake pattern.

We were about to start on a cruise down a river which the lumbermen said could not be "run," as it was shallow and rocky. We could find no one who had been down it, and so, not knowing anything about it, we regarded it as a pleasant prospect. Harrison, being a professional guide and hunter, had mostly come in contact with people—or "sports," as he called them, who had no sooner entered the woods than they were overcome with a desire to slay. No fatigue or exertion was too great when the grand purpose was to kill the deer and despoil the trout streams, but to go wandering aimlessly down a stream which by general consent was impracticable for boats, and then out into the clearings where the mountain-spring was left behind, and where logs and mill-dams and agriculturists took the place of the deer and the trout, was a scheme which never quite got straightened out in his mind. With many misgivings, and a very clear impression that I was mentally deranged, "Has" allowed that "we're all aboard."

We pushed out into the big lake and paddled. As we skirted the shores the wind howled through the giant hemlocks, and the ripples ran

BLACK WATER AND SHALLOWS

COPYRIGHT 1905 BY P. F. COLLIER & SON

away into whitecaps on the far shore. As I wielded my double-blade paddle and instinctively enjoyed the wildness of the day, I also indulged in a conscious calculation of how long it would take my shirt to dry on my back. It is such a pity to mix a damp shirt up with the wild storm, as it hurries over the dark woods and the black water, that I felt misgivings; but, to be perfectly accurate, they divided my attention, and, after all, man is only noble by fits and starts.

We soon reached the head of the river, and a water-storage dam and a mile of impassable rapids made a "carry" or "portage" necessary. Slinging our packs and taking the seventy-pound canoe on our shoulders, we started down the trail. The torture of this sort of thing is as exquisitely perfect in its way as any ever devised. A trunk-porter in a summer hotel simply does for a few seconds what we do by the hour, and as for reconciling this to an idea of physical enjoyment, it cannot be done. It's a subtle mental process altogether indefinable; but your enthusiast is a person who would lose all if he reasoned any, and to suffer like an anchorite is always part of a sportsman's programme. The person who tilts back in a chair on the veranda of a summer hotel, while he smokes cigars and gazes vacantly into space, is your only true philosopher; but he is not a sportsman. The woods and the fields and the broad roll of the ocean do not beckon to him to come out among them. He detests all their sensations, and believes nothing holy except the dinner hour, and with his bad appetite that too is flat, stale and unprofitable. A real sportsman, of the nature-loving type, must go tramping or paddling or riding about over the waste places of the earth, with his dinner in his pocket. He is alive to the terrible strain of the "carry," and to the quiet pipe when the day is done. The camp-fire contemplation, the beautiful quiet of the misty morning on the still water, enrapture him, and his eye dilates, his nerves tingle, and he is in a conflagration of ecstasy. When he is going—going—faster—faster into the boil of the waters, he hears the roar and boom ahead, and the black rocks crop up in thickening masses to dispute his way. He is fighting a game battle with the elements, and they are remorseless. He may break his leg or lose his life in the tip-over which is imminent, but the fool is happy—let him die.

But we were left on the "carry," and it is with a little thrill of joy and the largest sigh of relief possible when we again settle the boat in the water. Now you should understand why it is better to have one shirt and wash it often. My "canoe kit" is the best arranged and the most perfect in the world, as no other canoeist will possibly admit, but which nevertheless is a fact. One blanket, a light shelter-tent, a cooking outfit, which folds up in a sort of Japanese way, a light axe, two canvas packs, and tea, bacon and flour. This does not make long reading, but it makes a load for a man when it's all packed up, and a canoeist's baggage must be cut to the strength of his back. It is a great piece of confidence in which I will indulge you when I caution you not to pick out invalids for canoe companions. If a burro would take kindly to back woods navigation, I should enjoy the society of one, though it would not be in the nature of a burro to swing an axe, as indeed there are many fine gentlemen who cannot do a good job at that; and if one at least of the party cannot, the camp-fires will go out early at nights, and it is more than probable that the companions will have less than twenty toes between them at the end of the cruise.

All these arrangements being perfected, you are ready to go ahead, and in the wilderness you have only one anxiety, and that is about the "grub." If the canoe turn over, the tea, the sugar, and the flour will mix up with the surrounding elements, and only the bacon will remain to nourish you until you strike the clearings, and there are few men this side 70° north latitude who will gourmandize on that alone.

The long still water is the mental side of canoeing, as the rapid is the life and movement. The dark woods tower on either side, and the clear banks, full to their fat sides, fringed with trailing vines and drooping ferns, have not the impoverished look of civilized rivers. The dark water wells along, and the branches droop to kiss it. In front the gray sky is answered back by the water reflection, and the trees lie out as though hung in the air, forming a gateway, always receding. Here and there an old monarch of the forest has succumbed to the last blow and fallen across the stream. It reaches out ever so far with its giant stems, and the first branch had started sixty feet from the ground. You may have to chop a way through, or you may force your canoe through the limbs and gather a crowd of little broken branches to escort you along the stream. The original forest tree has a character of its own, and I never see one but I think of the artist who drew second-growth timber and called it "the forest primeval." The quietness of the woods, with all their solemnity, permitting no bright or overdressed plant to obtrude itself, is rudely shocked by the garish painted thing as the yellow polished Necoochee glides among them. The water-rat dives with a tremendous splash as he sees the big monster glide by his sedge home. The kingfisher springs away from his perch on the dead top with loud chatterings when we glide into his notice. The crane takes off from his grassy "set back" in a deliberate manner, as though embarking on a tour to Japan, a thing not to be hurriedly done. The mink eyes you from his sunken log, and, grinning in his most savage little manner, leaps away. These have all been disturbed in their wild homes as they were about to lunch off the handiest trout, and no doubt they hate us in their liveliest manner; but the poor trout under the boat compensate us with their thanks. The mud-turtle is making his way up-stream, as we can tell by the row of bubbles which arise in his wake, and the "skaters," as I call the little insects which go skipping about like a lawyer's point in an argument, part as we go by. The mosquotoes, those despirate little villains who dispute your happiness in the woods, are there, but they smell the tar and oil of our war paint, and can only hum in their anger. A stick cracks in the brush, and with all the dash and confidence of a city girl as she steps from her front door, a little spotted fawn walks out on a sedge bank from among the alders. He does not notice us, but in his stupid little way looks out to the freshest water-grass, and the hunter in the stern of the boat cuts his paddle through the water, and the canoe glides silently up until right under his nose. We are still and silent. The little thing raises its head and looks us full in the eye, and then continues to feed as before. I talk to him quietly, and say, "Little man, do not come near the pond or the rivers, for you will not live to have five prongs on your antlers if any one but such good people as we see you." He looks up, and seems to say, "You are noisy, but I do not care." "Now run; and if you ever see anything in the forest which resembles us, run for your life;" and with a bound the little innocent has regained the dark aisles of the woods. You loll back on your pack, your pipe going lazily; your hat is off; you moralize, and think thoughts which have dignity. You drink in the spell of the forest, and dream of the birch barks and the red warriors who did this same thing a couple of centuries since. But as thoughts vary so much in individuals, and have but an indirect bearing on canoeing, I will proceed without them. The low swamp, with its soft timber, gives place to hills and beech ridges, and the old lord of the forest for these last hundred years towers up majestically. The smaller trees fight for the sunlight, and thus the ceaseless war of nature goes on quietly, silently, and alone. The miserable "witch-hoppel" leads its lusty plebeian life, satisfied to spring its half-dozen leaves, and not dreaming to some day become an oak. The gentle sigh of the forest, the hum of insects, and the chatter and peal of the birds have gone into harmony with a long, deep, swelling sound, becoming louder and louder, until finally it drowns all else.

The canoe now glides more rapidly. The pipe is laid to one side. The paddle is grasped firmly, and with a firm eye I regard the "grub" pack which sits up in the bow, and resolve to die if necessary in order that it may not sink if we turn over. The river turns, and the ominous growl of the rapids is at hand.

"Hold her—hold her now—to the right of the big rock; and then swing to the far shore: if we go to the right, we are gone."

"All right; let her stern come round," and we drop away.

No talking now, but with every nerve and muscle tense, and your eye on the boil of the water, you rush along. You back water and paddle, the stern swings, she hangs for an instant, she falls in the current, and with a mad rush you take it like a hunting-man a six-bar gate. Now paddle, paddle, paddle. It looks bad—we cannot make it—yes—all right, and we are on the far shore, with the shallows on the other side. This little episode was successful, but, as you well know, it cannot last. The next rift, and with a bump she is hung upon a sunken rock, and—jump! jump!—we both flounder overboard in any way possible, so it is well and quickly done. One man loses his hold, the other swings the boat off, and kicking and splashing for a foothold, the demoralized outfit shoots along. At last one is found, and then at a favorable rock we embark again.

You are now wet, but the tea and sugar are safe, so it's a small matter. A jam of logs and tops is "hung up" on a particularly nasty place, and you have a time getting the boat around it. You walk on rotten tops while the knots stick up around you like sabres. "Has" floats calmly out to sea as it were on a detached log which he is cutting, and with a hopeless look of despair he totters, while I yell, "Save the axe,—you—save the axe!" and over he goes, only to get wet and very disgusted, both of which will wear off in time. For a mile the water is so shallow that the boat will not run loaded, and we lead her along as we wade, now falling in over our heads, sliding on slippery stones, hurting our feet, wondering why we had come at all. The boat gets loose, and my heart stands still as the whole boat-load of blankets and grub with our pipes and tobacco started off for the settlements —or "drifting to thunder," as Bret Harte said of Chiquita. There was a rather lively and enthusiastic pursuit instituted then, the details of which are forgotten, as my mind was focused on the grub-pack, but we got her. About this time the soles let go on my tennis shoes, and my only pair of trousers gave way. These things, however, became such mere details as to be scarcely noticed when you have traveled since sunrise up to your waist in water, and are tired, footsore, and hungry. It is time to go ashore and camp.

You scrape away a rod square of dirt, chunks, witch-hoppel, and dead leaves, and make a fire. You dry your clothes while you wear the blanket and the guide the shelter-tent, and to a casual observer it would look as though the savage had come again; but he would detect a difference, because a white man in a blanket is about as inspiring a sight as an Indian with a plug-hat.

Finally the coffee boils, the tent is up, and the bough bed laid down. You lean against the dead log and swap lies with the guide; and the greatest hunters I have ever known have all been magnificent liars. The two go together. I should suspect a man who was deficient. Since no one ever believes hunters' yarns, it has come to be a pleasurable pastime, in which a man who has not hunted considerably cannot lie properly without offending the intelligence of that part of his audience who have.

The morning comes too soon, and after you are packed up and the boat loaded, if you are in a bad part of the river you do this: you put away your pipe, and with a grimace and a shudder you step out into the river up to your neck and get wet. The morning is cold, and I, for one, would not allow a man who was perfectly dry to get into my boat, for fear he might have some trepidation about getting out promptly if the boat was "hung up" on a rock; and in the woods all nature is subservient to the "grub."

Hour after hour we waded along. A few rods of still water and "Has" would cut off large chews of tobacco, and become wonderfully cynical as to the caprices of the river. The still water ends around the next point. You charge the thing nobly, but end up in the water up to your neck with the "grub" safe, and a mile or so more of wading in the prospect.

Then the river narrows, and goes tumbling off down a dark canon cut through the rocks. We go ashore and "scout the place," and then begin to let the boat down on a line. We hug the black sides like ants, while the water goes to soapsuds at our feet. The boat bobs and rocks, and is nearly upset in a place where we cannot follow it through. We must take it up a ledge about thirty feet high, and after puffing and blowing and feats of maniacal strength, we at last have it again in the water. After some days of this thing we found from a statistician we had dropped 1100 feet in about fifty-one miles, and with the well known propensity of water to flow down hill, it can be seen that difficulties were encountered. You cannot carry a boat in the forest, and you will discover enough reasons why in a five-minute trail to make their enumeration tiresome. The zest of the whole thing lies in not knowing the difficulties beforehand, and then, if properly equipped, a man who sits at a desk the year through can find no happier days than he will in his canoe when the still waters run through the dark forest and the rapid boils below. ■ ■

THE PORTAGE

STUBBLE AND SLOUGH IN DAKOTA

Stubble and Slough in Dakota

The following story first appeared in Harper's *New Monthly Magazine*, August, 1894, and was also included in *Pony Tracks*.

Now I am conscious that all my life I have seen men who owned shot-guns and setter-dogs, and that these persons were wont at intervals to disappear from their usual haunts with this paraphernalia. Without thinking, I felt that they went to slay little birds, and for them I entertained a good-natured contempt. It came about in this wise that I acquired familiarity with "mark" and "hie-on" and "No. 6 vis No. 4's": By telegram I was invited to make one of a party in Chicago, bound west on a hunting expedition. It being one of my periods of unrest, I promptly packed up my Winchester, boots, saddle and blankets, wired "All right—next train," and crawled into the "Limited" at Forty-second Street.

"West" is to me a generic term for that country in the United States which lies beyond the high plains, and this will account for my surprise when I walked into the private car at the St. Paul depot in Chicago and met my friends contesting the rights of occupancy with numerous setter-dogs, while all about were shot-gun cases and boxes labeled "Ammunition." After greetings I stepped to the station platform and mingled with the crowd—disgusted and disposed to desert.

A genial young soldier who appreciated the curves in my character followed me out, and explained, in the full flush of his joyous anticipation, that we were going to North Dakota to shoot ducks and prairie-chicken, and that it would be the jolliest sort of time; besides, it was a party of good friends. I hesitated, yielded, and enlisted for the enterprise. Feeling now that I was this far it would be good to go on and learn what there was in the form of sport which charmed so many men whose taste I respected in other matters, and once embarked I summoned my enthusiasm, and tried to "step high, wide and handsome," as the horsemen say.

The happiness of a hunting party is like that of a wedding, so important is it that true love shall rule. The piece de resistance of our car was two old generals, who called each other by an abbreviation of their first names, and interrupted conversations by recalling to each other's memory where some acres of men were slain. "A little more of the roast beef, please—yes, that was where I was shot in this side;" and at night, when quiet reigned and we sought sleep, there would be a waving of the curtains, and a voice, "Oh, say, Blank, do you remember that time my horse was hit with the twelve-pounder?" and it banished dreams. There was a phlebotomist from Pittsburgh who had shot all over the earth. He was a thorough sportsman, with a code of rules as complicated as the common law, and he "made up tough" in his canvas shooting clothes. There was a young and distinguished officer of the regular army who had hunted men, which excused him in the paltry undertaking before him; and, finally, three young men who were adding the accumulated knowledge of Harvard to their natural endowments. For myself, I did not see how jack-boots, spurs and a Winchester would lend themselves to the stubble and slough of Dakota, but a collection was taken, and by the time we arrived in Valley City, Dakota, I was armed, if not accoutred, in the style affected by double-barrel men. All I now needed was an education, and between the Doctor, who explained, expostulated, and swore, and a great many "clean misses," I wore on to the high school stage. Like the obliging person who was asked if he played on the violin, I said to myself, "I don't know, but I'll try."

In the early morning three teams drove up where our car was side-tracked, and we embarked in them. The shot-gun man affects buck-colored canvas clothes, with many pockets, and carries his cartridges in his shirt fronts, like a Circassian Cossack. He also takes the shells out of his gun before he climbs into a wagon, or he immediately becomes an object of derision and dread, or, what's worse, suddenly friendless and alone. He also refrains from pointing his gun at any fellow-sportsman, and if he inadvertently does it, he receives a fussilade such as an Irish drill-sergeant throws into a recruit when he does amiss. This day was cool and with a wind blowing, and the poor dogs leaped in delirious joy when let out from their boxes, in which they had traveled all the way from Chicago. After running the wire edge off from their nerves they were gotten to range inside a township site, and we jogged along. The first thing which interested me was to hear the Doctor indicate to the driver that he did not care to participate in the driver's knowledge of hunting, and that in order to save mental wear he only had to drive the team, and stand fast when he got out, in order that from the one motionless spot on the prairie sea we could "mark down" the birds.

The immensity of the wheat fields in Dakota is astonishing to a stranger. They begin on the edge of town, and we drive all day and are never out of them, and on either side they stretch away as far as one's eye can travel. The wheat had been cut and "shocked" which left a stubble some eight inches high. The farm houses are far apart, and, indeed, not often in sight, but as the threshing was in progress, we saw many groups of men and horses, and the great steam-threshers blowing clouds of black smoke, and the flying straw as it was belched from the bowels of the monsters.

During the heat of the day the chickens lie in the cover of the grass at the sides of the fields, or in the rank growth of some slough-hole, but at early morning and evening they feed in the wheat stubble. As we ride along, the dogs range out in front, now leaping gracefully along, now stopping and carrying their noses in the air to detect some scent, and finally —"There's a point! Stop, driver!" and we pile out, breaking our guns and shoving in the cartridges.

"No hurry—no hurry," says the Doctor; "the dog will stay there a month." But, fired with the anticipations, we move briskly up. "You take the right and I'll take the left. Don't fire over the dog," adds the portly sportsman, with an admonishing frown. We go more slowly, and suddenly, with a "whir," up get two chickens and go sailing off. Bang! Bang! The Doctor bags his and I miss mine. We load and advance, when up comes the remainder of the covey, and the bewildering plenty of the flying objects rattles me. The Doctor shoots well, and indeed prairie-chickens are not difficult, but I am discouraged. As the great sportsman Mr. Soapy Sponge used to say, "I'm a good shooter but a bad hitter." It was in this distressful time that I remembered the words of the old hunter who had charge of my early education in .45 calibres, which ran, "Take yer time, sonny, and always see your hind sight," and by dint of doing this I soon improved to a satisfactory extent. The walking over the stubble is good exercise, and it becomes fascinating to watch the well trained Llewellyn setters "Make game," or stand pointing with their tails wagging violently in the nervous thrill of their excitement, then the shooting, and the marking down of the birds who escape the fire, that we may go to them for another flush. With care and patience one can bag at least the whole covey.

At noon we met the other wagons in a green swale, and had lunch, and, seated in a row under the shadow side of a straw stack, we plucked chickens, while the phlebotomist did the necessary surgery to prepare them for the cook. At three o'clock the soldier, a couple of residents and myself started together for the evening shooting. We banged away at one-thousand yards' range at some teal on a big marsh, but later gave it up, and confined ourselves to chicken. In the midst of a covey and a lot of banging I heard the Captain uttering distressful cries. His gun was leaning on a wheat "shock" and he was clawing himself wildly. "Come help me—I am being eaten alive." Sure enough he was, for in Dakota there is a little insect which is like a winged ant, and they go in swarms, and their bite is sharp and painful. I attempted his rescue, and was attacked in turn, so that we ended by a precipitous retreat, leaving the covey of chickens and their protectors, the ants, on the field.

We next pushed a covey of grouse into some standing oats, and were tempted to go in a short way, but some farmers who were thrashing on a neighboring hill blew on the engine whistle and made a sortie, whereat we bolted. At a slough which we were tramping through to kick up some birds "marked down," one suddenly got up under our feet and flew directly over the Captain, who yelled "Don't shoot!" as he dropped to the ground. It was a well considered thing to do, since a flying bird looks bigger than a man to an excited and enthusiastic sportsman. We walked along through the stubble until the red sunset no longer gave sufficient light, and then got into our wagons to do the fourteen miles to our car and supper. Late at night we reached our car, and from it could hear "the sound of revelry." The cook did big Chicago beefsteaks by the half-dozen, for an all day tramp is a sauce which tells.

After some days at this place we were hauled up to Devil's Lake, on the Great Northern road, which locality is without doubt the best for duck shooting in Dakota. We were driven some sixteen miles to a spur of the lake where we found a settler. There were hundreds of teal in the water back of his cabin, and as we took position well up the wind and fired, they got up in clouds. We gave the "bag" to the settler, and the Doctor admonished him to "fry them" which I have no doubt he did.

It was six miles to a pond said to be the best evening shooting about there, and we drove over. There we met our other two teams and another party of sportsmen. The shallow water was long and deeply fringed with rank marsh grass. Having no wading boots can make no difference to a sportsman whose soul is great, so I floundered in and got comfortably wet. After shooting two or three mud-hens, under the impression that they were ducks, the Doctor came along, and with a pained expression he carefully explained what became of people who did not know a teal from a mud-hen, and said further that he would let it pass this time. As the sun sank, the flight of ducks began and from the far corners of the marsh I saw puffs of smoke and heard the dull slump of a report.

"Mark—left," came a voice from where the young Harvard man with the peach complexion and the cream hair had ensconced himself in the grass, and, sure enough, a flight was coming toward my lair. I waited until it was nearly over when I rose up and missed two fine shots while the Harvard man scored. The birds fell well out in the pond and he waded out to retrieve them.

As I stood there the soft ooze of the marsh gradually swallowed me, and when in answer to the warning "mark," of my fellows I squatted down in the black water to my middle, and only held my gun and cartridges up, I began to realize that when a teal-duck is coming down wind you have got to aim somewhere into the space ahead of it, hoping to make a connection between your load of shot and the bird. This I did, and after a time got my first birds. The air was now full of flying birds—mallards, spoon-bills, pintails, red-heads, butter-balls, gadwalls, widgeon and canvas backs.

The sun has set and no longer bathes the landscape in its golden light. We give over at last and the fortunates change their wet clothes while those who have no change sit shivering while we rattle homeward. Our driver gets himself lost and we bring up against a wire fence. Very late at night we struck the railroad and counted telegraph poles and traveled east until the lights of the town twinkled through the gloom. Once in the car we find the creature comfort which reconciles one to life and we voted the day a red letter one. The goose shooting came later than our visit but the people tell marvelous tales of their numbers. They employ special guns in their pursuit, which are No 4. gauge, single-barreled, and very long. They throw buckshot pointblank two-hundred yards and are, indeed, curious looking arms.

The car was to be attached to an express train bound west that night, to my intense satisfaction, and I crawled into the upper berth to dream of bad-lands elk, soldiers, cowboys, and only in the haze of fleeting consciousness could I distinguish a voice—

"Remington, I hope you are not going to fall out of that upper berth again to-night." ■ ■

WINTER SHOOTING ON THE GULF COAST OF FLORIDA

Winter Shooting
on the Gulf Coast of Florida

This short article appeared in *Harper's Weekly*, May 11, 1895.

A T THAT PERIOD OF THE YEAR when the bad old lung and the inflamed bronchial tube and the festive catarrh get in their work, the fellow who likes to be amused goes off to the Mediterranean, and the fellow who likes to amuse himself hies him to Florida.

There is no reason why anyone should go to Cuba, so far as I can see, and Arizona is as yet not properly appreciated by "lungers" and sportsmen as a winter resort, although it is the superior place.

This Florida sportsman goes down on the Gulf coast because there is no doubt that in remote times of the past men have caught tarpon there. He may even desire to participate in the sensations which are said to have been so dear to the tarpon fisherman when the world was young. He may even hire a boat and a darky and go up some desolate inlet and sit quietly for ten hours while the clouds roll overhead, the wind plays through the reeds, and the darky perspires quietly in the forward end of the boat; but if he has got a nerve in his body he will shortly consign tarpon to his Satanic Majesty, pull up his anchor, go back to the hotel, sell his rod and tackle to some newly arrived enthusiast, and get out his twelve-bore.

Ducks down there are confiding birds, and a boat loaded with girls, and grub and Scotch whisky and soda can be sailed right up to them while the sportsman empties his shot-gun and fills his game-bag.

Then if he has a pointer-dog he can kick up quail, or wander among the sloughs or along the beaches and bang away at the illusive jack-snipe, and if he ever hits one he can plume himself on his skill as much as he likes, but he should properly attribute it to good luck. ■ ■

81

In the July 1895 issue of Harper's *New Monthly Magazine* there
appeared a story written and illustrated by Remington entitled
"Bear Chasing In The Rocky Mountains," the last of a group of
fifteen stories comprising his famous book *Pony Tracks*.

In this story Remington describes a hunt which took place on the
vast property of a rancher, Montague Stevens. In 1942 Mr. Stevens
wrote a book, *Meet Mister Grizzly*, part of which was devoted to
this particular incident. He writes that General Nelson A. Miles,
Chief of Staff of the United States Army, arrived with an escort
of cavalry from Fort Wingate together with a large party of friends
among whom were Leonard Wood and Frederic Remington.

General Miles, in his book *Personal Recollections and Observations*[10] also devotes a portion of Chapter 8 to this particular incident.

"There is, however, no rarer sport to me than hunting the bear
with a well trained pack of dogs. Mr. Montague Stevens of New
Mexico had, with a few of my own, a fine pack of dogs, composed
of blood hounds, fox terriers, stag hounds, boarhounds, and Russian
wolfhounds. The first were used as trailers, and taken altogether
they would tree or bring to bay any bear found in that country. In
fact they fought the bear so furiously that he would pay little attention to the hunters, and permit them to approach with compara-
tive safety. The hunters are usually mounted on strong, hardy, sure-
footed horses, as they are obliged to ride rapidly up and down the
sides of precipitous mountains. The mountains in that part of the

---

[10] The Werner Company, Chicago, 1896. In this book Remington made one of his
great contributions to western illustration.

country range from seven to ten thousand feet above sea-level, and are covered with scattering pine and cedar trees, with many rocks and ledges. Bear hunting is the most dangerous of all kinds of sport, and is uninteresting unless one is equipped with a well-trained pack of dogs; a pack used for no other purpose. Such dogs are never allowed to hunt any other game, such as deer or elk."

In the spring of 1896 Mr. Stevens visited New York and called upon Remington. Theodore Roosevelt, then Commissioner of Police of the City of New York, was a close personal friend of Remington's and it is a well known fact that he was a great sportsman. Remington suggested to Stevens that they pay Roosevelt a visit and so made their way down to Mulberry Street. Their conversation came around to bear hunting at which Roosevelt showed a keen interest and plans were made for a trip to New Mexico the following fall. During the elapsed period Mr. Stevens's entire dog pack was poisoned and the trip was cancelled. It never did occur.

Remington remarks in the following story that "A man will travel three thousand miles to kill a bear, not for love, or fear, or hate, or meat; for what then?"

It seems as if his thoughts were prophetic, that the day would come when in these very mountains where the grizzly had been so plentiful not one would remain. Men pursued him, advancing peoples drove him deeper and deeper into the wilderness until there was no-where to go, and there he died. It might be said of the grizzly that he alone remains, above all other animals, to link our world with that of the Old West. It was he, that the prospector, freighter and mountainman loved to talk about around the evening fire. They weaved their tales out of truths, imagination and pure downright fabrication. The stories they narrated were told and retold with new twists and highlights added.

In the *Century Magazine*, November 1890, Charles Howard Shinn had this to say, "Sometime, I am sure, an American Thorwaldsen will know how to hew an American grizzly out of some gray cliff of Rocklin granite, and there it will remain while the world endures, supreme as the Lion of Lucerne. Some day the hills will be empty of gold; the waters will have reclaimed the deserts; new conditions of life may have come to pass over all the lands from Maine to California. But every child will hear the story of old-world dragons and new-world grizzlies."

And so to Frederic Remington's story of "Bear Chasing In The Rocky Mountains."

GONE AWAY

Bear Chasing
in the Rocky Mountains

MR. MONTAGUE STEVENS IS AN ENGLISHMAN who for the most part attends to the rounding up of his cattle, which are scattered over the northwestern quarter of New Mexico; but he does not let that interfere with the time which all Englishmen set duly apart to be devoted to sport. His door-yard is some hundreds of miles of mountain wilderness and desolate mesa—a more gorgeous preserve than any king ever dreamed of possessing for his pleasure—with its plains dotted with antelope, and its mountains filled with cougar, deer, bear and wild turkeys. The white race has given up the contest with nature in those parts, and it has reverted to the bear, the Navajo, and Mr. Stevens, land grants, corrals, cabins, brands and all else.

General Miles was conducting a military observation of the country, which is bound to be the scene of any war which the Apaches or Navajos may make, and after a very long day's march, during which we had found but one water, and that was a pool of rain water, stirred into mud and full of alkali, where we had to let our horses into the muddy stuff at the ends of our lariats, we had at last found a little rivulet and some green grass. The coffee-pot bubbled and the frying-pan hissed, while I smoked, and listened to a big escort-wagon-driver who was repairing his lash, and say-

85

ing, softly, "Been drivin' a bloody lot of burros for thirty years, and don't know enough to keep a whip out of a wheel; guess I'll go to jack-punchin', 'nen I kin use a dry club."

Far down the valley a little cloud of dust gleamed up against the gray of the mountains, and presently the tireless stride of a pony shown darkly in its luminous midst. Nearer and nearer it grew—the flying tail, the regular beating of the hoofs, the swaying figure of the rider, and the left sleeve of the horseman's coat flapping purposely about. He crossed the brook with a splash, trotted, and, with a jerk, pulled up in our midst. Mr. Stevens is a tall, thin young man, very much bronzed, and with the set, serious face of an Englishman. He wore corduroy clothes, and let himself out of his saddle with one hand, which he also presented in greeting, the other having been sacrificed to his own shot-gun on some previous occasion. Mr. Stevens brought with him an enthusiasm for bear which speedily enveloped the senses of our party, and even crowded out from the mind of General Miles the nobler game which he had affected for thirty years.

The steady cultivation of one subject for some days is bound to develop a great deal of information, and it is with difficulty that I refrain from herein setting down facts which can doubtless be found in any good encyclopaedia of natural history; but the men in the mountains never depart from the consideration of that and one other subject, which is brands, and had reached some strange conclusions, the strangest being that the true Rocky Mountain grizzly is only seen once in a man's lifetime, and the biggest one they ever heard of leaves his tracks in this district, and costs Mr. Stevens, roughly estimating, about four hundred sixteen dollars a year to support, since that about covers the cattle he kills.

At break of day the officers, cavalrymen, escort wagons, and pack-train toiled up the Canon Largo to Mr. Stevens's camp, which was reached in good time, and consisted of a regular ranchman's grub-wagon, a great many more dogs of more varieties than I could possibly count, a big Texan, who was cook, and a professional bear-hunter by the name of Cooper, who had recently departed from his wonted game for a larger kind, with the result that after the final deal a companion had passed a .45 through Mr. Cooper's face and filled it with powder, and brought him nigh unto death, so that even now Mr. Cooper's head was swathed in bandages, and his mind piled with regrets that he had on at the time an overcoat, which prevented him from drawing his gun with his usual precision. Our introduction to the outfit was ushered in by a most magnificent free-for-all dog-fight; and when we had carefully torn the snarling, yelling, biting mass apart by the hind legs and staked them out to surrounding trees, we had time to watch Mr. Cooper draw diagrams of bear paws in the dust with a stick. These tracks he had just discovered up the Largo Canon, and he averred that the bear was a grizzly, and weighed eighteen hundred pounds, and that he had been there two years, and that all the boys had hunted him, but that he was a sad old rascal.

After lunch we pulled on up the canon and camped. The tents were pitched and the cooks busy, when I noticed three cowboys down the stream and across the canon who were alternately leading their horses and stooping down in earnest consultation over some tracks on the ground. We walked over to them. There were Mr. Cooper, whose only visible eye rolled ominously, and Dan, the S. U. foreman, with another puncher.

"He's usin' here," said Cooper. "That's his track, and there's his work," pointing up the hill-side, where lay the dead body of a five-year-old cow. We drew near her, and there was a tale of a mighty struggle all written out more eloquently than pen can do. There were the deep furrows of the first grapple at the top; there was the broad trail down the steep hill for fifty yards, with the stones turned over, and the dust marked with horn and hoof and claw; and there was the stump which had broken the roll down hill. The cow had her neck broken and turned under her body; her shoulder was torn from the body, her leg broken, and her side eaten into; and there was Bruin's big telltale footprints, rivaling in size a Gladstone bag, as he had made his way down to the stream to quench his thirst and continue up the canon. The cow was yet warm—not two hours dead.

"We must pull out of here; he will come back to-night," said Cooper. And we all turned to with a will and struck the tents, while the cooks threw their tins, bags, and boxes into the wagons, whereat we moved off down wind for three miles, up a spur of the canon, where we again camped. We stood around the fires and allowed Mr. Cooper to fill our minds with hope. "He'll shore come back; he's usin' here; an' cow outfits—why, he don't consider a cow outfit nothin'; he's been right on top of cow outfits since he's been in these parts, and thet two years gone now when he begun to work this yer range and do you see done yonder. In the mornin' we'll strike his trail, and if we can get to him you'll shore see a bar-fight."

We turned in, and during the night I was awakened twice, once by a most terrific baying of the dogs, who would not be quieted, and later by a fine rain beating in my face. The night was dark, and we were very much afraid the rain would kill the scent. We were up long before daylight, and drank our coffee and ate our meat, and as soon as "we could see a dog a hundred yards," which is the bear-hunter's receipt, we moved off down the creek. We found that the cow had been turned over twice, but not eaten; evidently Bruin had his suspicions. The dogs cut his trail again and again. He had run within sight of our camp, had wandered across the valley hither and yon, but the faithful old hounds would not "go away." Dan sat on his pony and blew his old cow's horn, and yelled, "Hooick! hooick! get down on him, Rocks; hooick! hooick!" But Rocks could not get down on him, and then we knew that the rain had killed the scent. We circled a

THE BEAR AT BAY

half-mile out, but the dogs were still; and then we followed up the Canon Largo for miles, and into the big mountain, through juniper thickets and over malpais, up and down the most terrible places, for we knew that the bear's bed-ground is always up in the most rugged peaks, where the rim-rock overhangs in serried battlements, tier on tier. But no bear.

Rocks, the forward hound, grew weary of hunting for things which were not, and retired to the rear for consultation with his mates; and Dan had to rope him, and with some irritation started the pony, and Rocks kept the pace by dint of legging it, and by the help of a tow from nine hundred pounds of horseflesh. Poor Rocks! He understood his business, but in consequence of not being able to explain to the men what fools they were, he suffered.

The hot mid-day sun of New Mexico soon kills the scent, and we were forced to give over for the day. A cavalry sergeant shot three deer, but we, in our superior purpose, had learned to despise deer. Later than this I made a good two-hundred-yard centre on an antelope, and though I had not been fortunate enough in years to get an antelope, the whole sensation was flat in view of this new ambition.

On the following morning we went again to our dead cow, but nothing except the jackals had been at the bear's prey, for the wily old fellow had evidently scented our camp, and concluded that we were not a cow outfit, whereat he had discreetly "pulled his freight."

We sat on our horses in a circle and raised our voices. In consideration of the time at our disposal, we concluded that we could be satisfied with taking eighteen hundred pounds of bear on the instalment plan. The first instalment was a very big piece of meat, but was, I am going to confess, presented to us in the nature of a gift; but the whole thing was so curious I will go into it.

We hunted for two days without success, unless I include deer and antelope; but during the time I saw two things which interested me. The first was a revelation of the perfect understanding which a mountain cow-pony has of the manner in which to negotiate the difficulties of the country which is his home.

Dan, the foreman, was the huntsman. He was a shrewd-eyed little, square-built man, always very much preoccupied with the matter in hand. He wore a sombrero modelled into much character by weather and time, a corduroy coat, and those enormous New Mexican "chaps," and he sounded a cow-horn for his dogs, and alternately yelped in a most amusing way. So odd was this yelp that it caught the soldiers, and around the camp-fire at night you could hear the mimicking shouts of, "Oh Rocks! eh-h-h! hooick! get down on him, Rocks; tohoot! tohoot!" We were sitting about on our horses in a little sienneca, while Dan was walking about, leading his pony and looking after his dogs.

When very near me he found it necessary to cross an arroyo which was about five feet deep and with perfectly perpendicular banks. Without hesitating, he jumped down into it, and, with a light bound, his pony followed. At the opposite side Dan put up his arms on the bank and clawed his way up, and still paying no attention to his pony, he continued on. Without faltering in the least, the little horse put his fore feet on the bank, clawed at the bank, once, twice, jumped, scratched, clawed, and, for all the world like a cat getting into the fork of a tree, he was on the bank and following Dan.

Later in the day, we followed one of Dan's short-cuts through the mountains, and the cowboys on their mountain ponies rode over a place which made the breath come short to the officers and men behind. Not that they could not cross themselves, being on foot, but that the cavalry horses could they had their solemn doubts, and no one but an evil brute desires to lead a game animal where he may lose his life. Not being a geologist, I will have to say it was a blue clay in process of rock formation, and in wet times held a mountain torrent. The slope was quite seventy degrees. The approach was loose dirt and malpais, which ran off down the gulch in small avalanches under our feet. While crossing, the horses literally stood on their toes to claw out a footing. A slip would have sent them, belly up, down the toboggan slide, with a drop into an unknown depth at the end. I had often heard the cavalry axiom "that a horse can go anywhere a man can if the man will not use his hands," and a little recruit murmured it to reassure himself. I passed with the loss with a quarter of the skin on my left hand, and later asked a quaint old veteran of four enlistments if he thought it was a bad place, and he said, "It's lizards, not harses, what ought to go thar."

Riding over the rough mountains all day sows poppy seeds in a man's head, and when the big medical officer opens your tent flaps in the morning, and fills the walls with his roars to "get up; it's four o'clock," it is with groans that you obey. You also forego washing, because you are nearly frozen stiff, and you go out and stand around the fire with your companions, who are all cheerfully miserable as they shiver and chaff each other. It seems we do not live this life on a cold calculating plane of existence, but on different lines, the variation of which is the chief delight of the discriminating, and I must record a distinct pleasure in elbowing fellows around a campfire when it is dark and cold and wet, and when you know that they are oftener in bed than out of it at such hours. You drink your quart of coffee, eat your slice of venison, and then regard your horse with some trepidation, since he is all of a tremble, has a hump on his back, and is evidently of a mind to "pitch."

The eastern sky grows pale, and the irrepressible Dan begins to "honk" on his horn, and the cavalcade moves off through the grease-wood, which sticks up thickly from the ground like millions of Omaha war-bonnets.

The advance consists of six or eight big blood-hounds, which range out in front, with Dan and Mr. Cooper to blow the horn, look out for "bear sign," and to swear gently but firmly when the younger dogs take recent deer trails under consideration. Three-hundred yards behind come Scotch stag-hounds, a big yellow mastiff, fox-terriers, and one or two dogs which would not classify in a bench show, and over these Mr. Stevens holds a guiding hand, while in a disordered band come General Miles, his son, three army officers, myself, and seven orderlies of the Second Cavalry. All this made a picture, but, like all western canvases, too big for a frame. The sun broke in a golden flash over the hills, and streaked the plain with gold and gray-greens. The spirit of the thing is not hunting but the chase of the bear, taking one's mind back to the buffalo, or the nobles of the Middle Ages, who made their "image of war" with bigger game than red foxes.

Leaving the plain, we wound up a dry creek, and noted that the small oaks had been bitten and clawed down by bear to get at the acorns. The hounds gave tongue, but could not get away until we had come to a small glade in the forest, where they grew wildly excited. Mr. Cooper here showed us a very large bear track, and also a smaller one, with those of two cubs by its side. With a wild burst the dogs went away up a canon, the blood went into our heads, and our heels into the horses, and a desperate scramble began. It is the sensation we have traveled so long to feel. Dan and Cooper sailed off through the brush and over the stones like two old crows, with their coat tails flapping like wings. We follow at a gallop in single file up the narrow dry watercourse. The creek ends, and we take to the steep hill-sides, while the loose stones rattle from under the flying hoofs. The rains have cut deep furrows on their way to the bed of the canon, and your horse scratches and scrambles for a foot-hold. A low gnarled branch bangs you across the face; and then your breath fairly stops as you see a horse go into the air and disappear over a big log fallen down a hill of seventy degrees' slope. The "take off and landing" is yielding dust, but the blood in your head puts the spur in your horse, and over you go. If you miss, it is a two-hundred-foot roll, with a twelve-hundred pound horse on top of you, but the pace soon tells, and you see nothing but good honest climbing ahead of you. The trail of the yelling dogs goes straight up, amid scraggly cedar and juniper, with malpais underfoot. We arrive at the top only to see Cooper and Dan disappear over a precipice after the dogs, but here we stop. Bears always seek the very highest peaks, and it is better to be there before them if possible. A grizzly can run down hill quicker than a horse, and all hunters try to get above them, since if they are big and fat they climb slowly; besides, the mountain tops are more or less flat and devoid of underbrush, which makes good running for a horse. We scatter out along the cordon of the range. The bad going on the rim-rock of the mountain tops, where the bear tries to throw off

KILLING A CATTLE THIEF

the dogs, makes it quite impossible to follow them at speed, so that you must separate, and take your chances of leading the chase.

I selected Captain Mickler—the immaculate—the polo-player—the epitome of staff form—the trappiest trooper in the Dandy Fifth, and, together with two orderlies, we started. Mickler was mounted on a cow-pony which measured one chain three links from muzzle to coupling. Mickler had on English riding togs—this is not saying that the pony could not run, or that Mickler was not humorous. But it was no new experience for him, this pulling a pony and coaxing him to attempt breakneck experiments, for he told me casually that he had led bare-footed cavalrymen over these hills in pursuit of Apaches at a date in history when I was carefully conjugating Latin verbs.

We were making our way down a bad formation, when we heard the dogs, and presently three shots. A strayed cavalry orderly had, much to his disturbance of mind, beheld a big silver-tip bearing down on him, jaws skinned, ears back, and red eyed, and he had promptly removed himself to a proper distance, where he dismounted. The bear and dogs were much exhausted, but the dogs swarmed around the bear, thus preventing a shot. But Bruin stopped at intervals to fight the dogs, and the soldier fired, but without effect. If men do not come up with the dogs in order to encourage them, many will draw off, since the work of chasing and fighting a bear without water for hours is very trying. The one now running was an enormous silver-tip, and could not "tree." The shots of the trooper diverted the bear, which now took off down a deep canon next to the one we were in, and presently we heard him no more. After an hour's weary traveling down the winding way we came out on the plain, and found a small cow-outfit belonging to Mr. Stevens, and under a tree lay our dead silver-tip, while a half dozen punchers squatted about it. It appeared that three of them had been working up in the foot-hills, when they heard the dogs, and shortly discovered the bear. Having no guns, and being on fairly good ground, they coiled their riatas and prepared to do battle.

The silver-tip was badly blown, and the three dogs that had stayed up with him were so tired that they sat up at a respectful distance and panted and lolled. The first rope went over Bruin's head and one paw. There lies the danger. But instantly number two flew straight to the mark, and the ponies surged, while Bruin stretched out with a roar. A third rope got his other hind leg, and the puncher dismounted and tied it to a tree. The roaring, biting, clawing mass of hair was practically helpless, but to kill him was an undertaking.

"Why didn't you brand him and turn him loose?" I asked of the cowboy.

"Well," said the puncher, in his Texas drawl, "we could have branded him all right, but we might have needed some help in turning him loose."

They pelted him with malpais, and finally stuck a knife into a vital part, and then, loading him on a pony, they brought him in. It was a daring performance, but was regarded by the punchers as a great joke.

Mickler and I rode into camp, thinking on the savagery of man. One never heard of a bear which traveled all the way from New Mexico to Chicago to kill a man, and yet a man will go three thousand miles to kill a bear—not for love, or fear, or hate, or meat; for what, then? But Mickler and I had not killed a bear, so we were easy.

One by one the tired hunters and dogs straggled into camp, all disappointed, except the dogs, which could not tell us what had befallen them since morning. The day following the dogs started a big black bear, which made a good run up a bad place in the hills, but with the hunters scrambling after in full cry. The bear treed for the dogs, but on sighting the horsemen he threw himself backward from the trunk, and fell fifteen feet among the dogs, which latter piled into him en masse, the little fox-terriers being particularly aggressive. It was a tremendous shakeup of black hair and pups of all colors, but the pace was too fast for Bruin, and he sought a new tree. One little foxie had been rolled over, and had quite a job getting his bellows mended. This time the bear sat on a limb very high up, and General Miles put a .50-calibre ball through his brain, which brought him down with a tremendous thump, when the pups again flew into him, and "wooled him," as the cowboys put it, to their hearts' content.

While our bear-hunting is not the thing we are most proud of, yet the method is the most sportsmanlike, since nothing but the most desperate riding will bring one up with the bear in the awful country which they affect. The anticipation of having a big silver-tip assume the aggressive at any moment is inspiriting. When one thinks of the enormous strength of the "silvertip," which can overpower the mightiest steer, and bend and break its neck or tear its shoulder from its body at a stroke, one is able to say, "Do not hunt a bear unless thy skin is not dear to thee." Then the dogs must be especially trained to run bear, since the country abounds in deer, and it is difficult to train dogs to ignore their sight and scent. The cowboys account for the number of the bear in their country from the fact that it is the old Apache and Navajo range, and the incoherent mind of the savage was impressed with the rugged mass of fur and the grinning jaws of the monster which crossed his path, and he was awed by the dangers of the encounter—arrow against claw. He came to respect the apparition, and he did not know that life is only sacred when in the image of the Creator. He did not discriminate as to the value of life, but, with his respect for death, there grew the speculation, which to him became a truth, that the fearsome beast was of the other world, and bore the lost souls of the tribe. He was a vampire; he was sacred. Oh Bear! ■ ■

Of all animals none was held in such high affection by Remington as the horse. During his entire career he constantly sketched and painted the horse in all of its movements and moods. He understood the animal as indeed few men have. It was this understanding coupled with his keen observation that will forever associate Remington's name with the horse. Perhaps, too, there was a profound sympathy with the lot of this second best of man's friends that enabled the artist to so magnificently portray this animal under all the conditions to which he was subjected. Early in his career Remington could foresee the road ahead for he wrote of the western bronco:

"This particular American horse lays claim to another quality which in my estimation is not least, and that is his wonderful picturesqueness. He graces the western landscape, not because he reminds us of the equine ideal, but because he comes of the soil, and has borne the heat and burden and the vicissitudes of all the pale of romance which will cling about the western frontier. As we see him hitched to the plow or the wagon he seems a living protest against the utilitarianism; but, unlike his red master he will not go. He has borne the Moor, the Spanish conqueror, the Indian, the mountain-man and the vaquero through all the glories of their careers; but they will soon be gone, with all their heritage of gallant deeds. The pony will meekly enter the new regime. He must wear the collar

96

of the new civilization and earn his oats by the sweat of his flanks. There are no more worlds for him to conquer."

This passage was written for Remington's "Horses of the Plains," published in the January 1889 issue of *Century Magazine*. As he prophesied, the horse has gradually passed from our way of life for modes of transportation more suited to progress. Though his glories are still very much alive—perhaps more so than ever before— in the world of sport.

Remington's fame was founded on his drawings and paintings of the horse in the western scene. His talents were also recognized and diverted to the illustrating of the horse in sport—the National Horse Show, the trotting track, the steeplechase, the bridle path and other events in which the horse played a major role.

On the following pages are reproduced a variety of these scenes.

Julian Ralph summed up this tribute to Remington and the horse when he wrote, "In one of the treaty ports of China, last autumn, the annual pony-races had been held, and some of the gentlemen riders were at a dinner which I attended. 'I only wish that Frederic Remington had seen one of the races to-day,' said one of the gentlemen. 'What? Do you know Remington?' I asked, in surprise. 'Know him?' answered two or three at once; 'I rather think we do.' And then the first speaker added, 'If only he could come out here and paint our ponies—well, they'd be properly done, that's all.'

"I hardly need say that he loves the horse, but what not everyone knows is that he has said he would be proud to have carved on his tombstone the simple sentence 'HE KNEW THE HORSE.' "

The following appeared in *Harper's Weekly*, November 16, 1895.

Getting Hunters in Horse Show Form

THERE MAY BE A FEW BICYCLES up in the Genesee Valley, but the persons who ride them do not expect to run for Congress in that district, because the people there ride horses, and awfully good ones too, for the most part. They talk horse and think horse, and even the women are wise as serpents concerning equine matters, enough to distress a Bull's Head dealer were one to go among them. As one goes about the country every now and then they will see in some stable a groom holding a horse by the head, while slowly walking about him is a group of men in boots or leggings, with possibly a woman or two, all silently intent on their observations, as if it were an ancient fresco on a conqueror's tomb on which they gazed. The countryside itself is one of the most delightful pastoral landscapes in America—much the impression of England—well farmed and prosperous. Set about in the hills are the fine country-seats of the Wadsworths, the Howlands, and others, backed by big stables, all the stalls blocked with hunters, the grounds cut up with hurdles, rails and water, stone walls and Liverpool jumps; and quite common to see are horses dancing over them as they take their exercise. One is made to wonder why there is not more of the same thing elsewhere in New York State, given up as it is to the production of gangling and nearly unsalable trotting stock. Any good horse of the hunter type, able to clear his five feet nicely, is gold in the hands of his owner. Many of the hunters come from Canada, up Toronto way, where years ago retired British army officers settled and raised horses from Irish hunter stock, which has made that country celebrated, and customers come in flocks to buy them. Unless a man rides at

99

SCHOOLING HUNTERS FOR THE HORSE SHOW

the very top weight he can be suited in his mount without importing from England or Ireland. The training of a hunter involves, first, a development of his jumping qualities in order to determine whether he will make a "hunter" or not, and on its being decided favorably, a stable boy may carry along his education until the finishing course which must or should be given him by the master who is to hunt him. To my astonishment, a very celebrated riding man told me that occasionally an American trotting horse turns out a crack hunter, but I cannot bring myself to think that much could be hoped for from such a quarter.

Many of the farmers up Genesee way breed hunters, ride them to hounds, and if the horse performs well they will sell out at a good sum to some of the gentlemen who run up there to hunt the country. When the Horse Show is on in New York great numbers of horses are shipped down to the city to participate in the contests, and many of these never return, being sold to other parts. Men who ride to hounds usually keep three horses for that purpose, and many keep more, while Mr. Howland has mounted fourteen visiting friends from his stable for one run. People are constantly changing their mounts, and naturally this buying and turning off of horses puts a man into a dealer's way almost. For one who wants a horse of that character what better can he do than to go right to the stables of the big hunting man? He may not acquire their top horses, but he can find tremendous hacks which are not up to the hunting man's ideas over the timber. As I have said, one can see the hunters being schooled over the timber, which is always a good show, and he can tell the "proper" from the "flying jumper," and see all the form, never forgetting that the groom who is "up" is likely to ride amazingly well. The younger horses are first whipped along a chute and forced over rails thickly padded with straw covered with burlaps, they are then mounted by boys, until some few finally develop to horse-show form and are entered for competition in the local show, which latter determines whether they are to command the plaudits of the multitude in the great Garden, or are simply to follow the pack over the quiet valley. I saw the gallant old Ontario brought out and put over the rails for the edification of some visitors, and he does it in his old workmanlike manner despite his lost eye and his years.

He is to be immortalized by the master, for Mr. St. Goudens has used the grand old fellow as a model in his statue of General Sherman. Who will say that horses cannot have careers, and grand ones too? For one, I might hesitate if I had to decide to be either Ontario or some one of the millions of human beings who are not up to man-show form. Fie on this thing called contentment! Ontario may have it, though it properly only belongs to Florida negroes and house-dogs. If my soul should ever transmigrate into a horse, let it be into a grand hunter's body—unbroken to harness, arched in the loin, high withers running far back, lean shoulders extended and play-

GETTING HUNTERS IN HORSE SHOW FORM

ing like a pugilist's arms, neck supple and far from the hand, tail set high, and quarters as large as a freight-car, with my forearm like a blacksmith's; then let me have pattens like the fencer's wrist, good long hard hoofs well open behind, and the head I must suppose to be my own. I will carry a gentleman over the country if his hands are light on my mouth and his seat is steady and well back; if we tangle up and turn over it is no more likely to hurt me than the fellow who rides me where I cannot go. If my master is a hard hunting man, I doubt not he will want me hard on the dogs, in which case I must hope he will have a cool head, and will help me out of the difficulties I have encountered in getting over the uneven ground, but by the tail of Bacephalus I hope he don't use his arms, except to steady me when I land badly or stumble on a rolling stone in some shifty going. Some men will become excited, and will not know as well as I how to negotiate the going, and if so—very well—I will leave him piled up in a ditch somewhere, waiting for whiskey and water and court-plaster, and go racing on after the hounds, where some better man who is riding up will see me and say it was not my fault, because he will know that my rider had no seat, because he could see that at the meet in the morning, where I kicked around a bit to loosen my sinews, and the good rider will buy me—in short, I will become possessed of a good master by my cleverness in the field; and once I have him, if he is really a good master, I will take him where he wants to go, and I will be so game that I will strain the last nerve—all to do the thing he puts me at. I may come to grief, but the good master, after he has put plaster on his nose and linament on his wrists, will turn over in his bed and say to himself, "I should not have put my heels into him at the last jump, because his nerves were dead, his legs heavy, and his stomach drawn into his wind." He will come out to see that the grooms rub embrocation on my knees, and repent of his ardor, while I will hope to get right in my knees as soon as he does in his wrists, whereupon we will play together some more.

Then at various times when I am a youngster I will win silver cups for him at the shows, and then in "mine age" he will not turn me off, because he will, after dinner, show his visiting friends the long row of big silver mugs on his mantel-piece, and they will all talk about me the evening through. All that will be good business. Of course he might lose his money on Wall Street. Then, if he was a good master, he would turn me off to some friend who also liked good hunters, and the cups on the mantel-piece would go with me. If he shouldn't do this I would kick the "stuffin'" out of any unsportsmanlike character who might come to possess me. I think, too, that none of these electrical sharps will ever invent a contraption to hunt the hounds, and so long as there are cows there will be fences. However, I shall never be a horse, or anything but—Frederic Remington. ■■

GOING TO THE HORSE SHOW

IN MADISON SQUARE GARDEN—ROAD COACHES IN THE RING

Lady Rider

Trotting Horse

Norman Percheron

Shetland Pony

Police Stopping Runaway

SKETCHES FROM THE HORSE SHOW
AT MADISON SQUARE GARDEN

Jumping Horse

Mare and Colt

107

A Gallery of
Remington Horses in Sport

A HUNTING MAN

110

TRAINING A YOUNG HUNTER

111

POLO-PLAYER

Copyright, 1890, by FREDERIC REMINGTON

JOCKEYS

113

INDIAN HORSE RACE—COMING OVER THE SCRATCH

114

A SOUTHERN RIDER

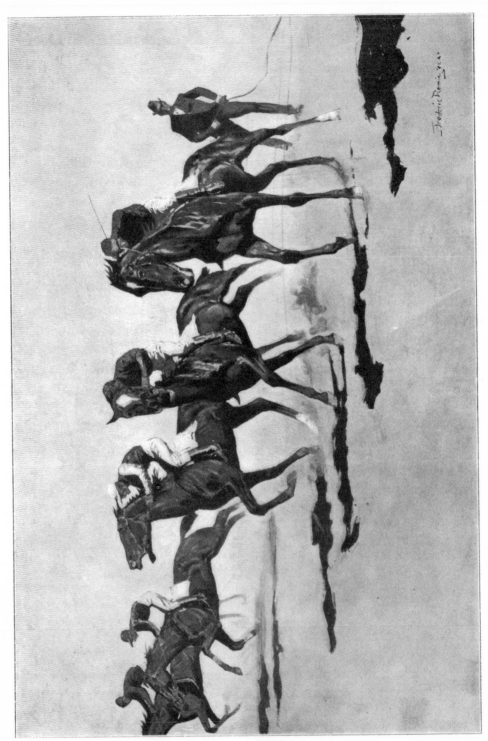

RACING

116

A FALSE START

A CLOSE FINISH

117

THE WATER JUMP AT CEDARHURST

Warming up. – a study of action.

Explaining defeat to the Owners.

A Break.

"You suah lose dat two dollars Jim"

Ready for a heat

SKETCHES FROM THE TROTTING TRACK

The Strange Days
that Came to Jimmie Friday

"The Strange Days that Came to Jimmie Friday" first appeared in Harper's *New Monthly Magazine*, August 1896 and was later included in Remington's books, *Crooked Trails* and *Stories of Peace and War*.

THE "ABWEE-CHEMUN" CLUB (Algonquin for paddle and canoe) was organized with six charter members at a heavy lunch in the Savarin Restaurant—one of those lunches which make through connections to dinner without change. One member basely deserted, while two more lost all their enthusiasm on the following morning, but three of us stuck. We vaguely knew that somewhere north of the Canadian Pacific and south of Hudson Bay were big lakes and rapid rivers—lakes whose names we did not know; lakes bigger than Champlain, with unnamed rivers between them. We did not propose to be boated around in a big birch-bark by two voyagers among blankets, and crackers and ham, but each provided himself with a little thirteen-foot cedar canoe, twenty-nine inches in the beam, and weighing less than forty pounds. I cannot tell you precisely how our party was sorted, but one was a lawyer with eye-glasses and settled habits, loving nature, though detesting canoes; the other was nominally a merchant, but in reality an atavic Norseman of the wolf and raven kind; while I am not new. Together we started.

Presently the Abwees sat about the board of a lumberman's hotel, filled with houseflies and slatternly waiter-girls, who talked familiarly while they

121

served greasy food. The Abwees were yet sore in their minds at the thoughts of the smelly beds upstairs, and discouragement sat deeply on their souls. But their time was not yet.

After breakfast they marched to the Hudson Bay Company's store, knowing as they did that in Canada there are only two places for a traveler to go if he wants anything—the great company or the parish priest; and then, they were told "that beyond, beyond some days' journey"—oh! that awful beyond, which for centuries has stood across the path of the pioneer, and in these latter days confronts the sportsman and wilderness-lover—"that beyond some days' journey to the north was a country such as they had dreamed—up Temiscamingue and beyond."

The subject of a guide was considered.

Jimmie Friday always brought a big toboggan-load of furs into Fort Tiemogamie every spring, and was accounted good in his business. He and his big brother trapped together, through the snow-laden forest which they had covered with their dead-falls and steel-jawed traps; but when the ice went out in the rivers, and the great pines dripped with the melting snows, they had nothing more to do then cut a few cords of wood for their widowed mother's cabin near the post. Then the brother and he paddled down to Bais des Pierres, where the brother engaged as a deck hand on a steamboat, and Jimmie hired himself as a guide for some bush-rangers, as the men are called who explore for pine lands for the great lumber firms. Having worked all summer and got through with that business, Jimmie bethought him to dissipate for a few days in the bustling lumber town down on the Ottawa River. He had been there before to feel the exhilaration of civilization, but beyond that clearing he had never known anything more inspiring than a Hudson Bay post, which is generally a log store, a house where the agent lives, a few tiny Indian cabins set higgledy-piggledy in a sunburnt gash of stumps and boulders, lost in the middle of the solemn, unresponsive forest. On this morning in question he had stepped from his friend's cabin up in the Indian village, and after lighting a perfectly round and rather yellow cigar, he had instinctively wandered to the Hudson Bay store, there to find himself amused by a strange sight.

The Abwees had hired two French-Indian voyagers of sinister mien, and a Scotch-Canadian boy bred to the bush. They were out on the grass, engaged in taking burlaps off three highly polished canoes, while the clerk from the store ran out and asked questions about "how much bacon," and, "will fifty pounds of pork be enough, sir?"

The round yellow cigar was getting stubby, while Jimmie's modest eyes sought out the points of interest in the new-comers, when he was suddenly and sharply addressed:

"Can you cook?"

Jimmy couldn't do anything in a hurry, except chop a log, paddle very fast, and shoot quickly, so he said, as was his wont,

"I think—I dun'no—"

"Well—how much?" came the query.

"Two daul-ars—" said Jimmie.

The transaction was complete. The yellow butt went over the fence, and Jimmie shed his coat. He was directed to lend a hand by the bustling sportsmen, and requested to run and find things of which he had never before in his life heard the name.

After two days' travel the Abwees were put ashore—boxes, bags, rolls of blankets, canoes, Indians, and plunder of many sorts—on a pebbly beach, and they backed off and turned away. They had reached the "beyond" at last, and the odoriferous little bedrooms, the bustle of the preparation, the cares of their lives, were behind. Then there was a girding up of the loins, a getting out of tump-lines and canvas packs, and the long portage was begun.

The voyagers each carried two-hundred pounds as they stalked away into the wilderness, while the attorney-at-law "hefted" his pack, wiped his eye-glasses with his pocket-handkerchief, and tried cheerfully to assume the responsibilities of "a dead game sport."

"I cannot lift the thing, and how I am going to carry it is more than I know; but I'm a dead-game sport, and I'm going to try. I do not want to be dead game yet, but it looks as though I couldn't help it. Will some gentleman help me to adjust this cargo?"

The night overtook the outfit in an old beaver meadow half-way through the trail. Like all first camps, it was tough. The lean-to tents went up awkwardly. No one could find anything. Late at night the Abwees lay on their backs under the blankets, while the fog settled over the meadow and blotted out the stars.

On the following day the stuff was all gotten through, and by this time the lawyer had become a voyager, willing to carry anything he could stagger under. It is strange how one can accustom himself to "pack." He may never use the tump-line, since it goes across the head, and will unseat his intellect if he does, but with shoulder-straps and a tump-line a man who thinks he is not strong will simply amaze himself inside of a week by what he can do. As for our little canoes, we could trot with them. Each Abwee carried his own belongings and his boat, which entitled him to the distinction of "a dead game sport," whatever that may mean, while the Indians portaged their larger canoes and our mass of supplies, making many trips backward and forward in the process.

At the river everything was parceled out and arranged. The birch-barks were repitched, and every man found out what he was expected to portage and do about camp. After breaking and making camp three times, the outfit could pack up, load the canoes, and move inside of fifteen minutes. At the first the lawyer essayed his canoe, and was cautioned the delicate thing might flirt with him. He stepped in and sat gracefully down in about two feet of water, while the "delicate thing" shook herself saucily at his side. After he had crawled dripping ashore and wiped his eye-glasses, he engaged to sell the "delicate thing" to an Indian for one dollar and a half on a promissory note. The trade was suppressed, and he was urged to try again. A man who has held down a cane-bottom chair conscientiously for fifteen years looks askance at so fickle a thing as a canoe twenty-nine inches in the beam. They are nearly as hard to sit on in the water as a cork; but once one is in the bottom they are stable enough, though they do not submit to liberties or palsied movements. The staid lawyer was filled with horror at the prospect of another go at his polished beauty; but remembering his resolve to be dead game, he abandoned his life to the chances, and got in this time safely.

So the Abwees went down the river on a golden morning, their double-blade paddles flashing the sun and sending the drip in a shower on the glassy water. The smoke from the lawyer's pipe hung behind him in the quiet air, while the note of the reveille clangored from the little buglette of the Norseman. Jimmie and the big Scotch backwoodsman swayed their bodies in one boat, while the two sinister voyagers dipped their paddles in the big canoe.

The Norseman's gorge came up, and he yelled back: "Say, this suits me. I am never going back to New York."

Jimmie grinned at the noise; it made him happy. Such a morning, such a water, such a lack of anything to disturb one's peace! let man's better na-ture revel in the beauties of existence; they inflate his soul. The colors play upon the senses—the reddish-yellow of the birch-barks, the blue of the water, and the silver sheen as it parts at the bows of the canoes; the dark evergreens, the steely rocks with their lichens, the white trunks of the birches, their fluffy tops so greeny green, and over all the gold of a sunny day. It is my religion, this thing, and I do not know how to tell all I feel concerning it.

The rods were taken out, and a gang of flies put on and trolled behind —but we have all seen a man fight a five-pound bass for twenty minutes. The waters fairly swarmed with them, and we could always get enough for the pot in a half hour's fishing at any time during the trip. The Abwees were canoeing, not hunting or fishing; though, in truth, they did not need to hunt spruce-partridge or fish for bass in any sporting sense; they simply went out after them and never stayed over half an hour. On a point we stopped for lunch: the Scotchman always struck the beach a-cooking. He had a "kit," which was a big camp-pail, and inside of it there were some more dishes than are to be found in some hotels. He broiled the bacon, instead of frying it, and thus we were saved the terrors of indigestion. He had many luxuries in his commissary, among them dried apples, with which he filled a camp-pail one day and put them on to boil. They subsequently got to be about a foot deep all over the camp, while Furguson stood around and regarded the black-magic of the thing with overpowering emotions and Homeric tongue. Furguson was a good genius, big and gentle, and a woodsman root and branch. The Abwees had their days in the wilderness to be happy singing flits of time, but with grease and paste in one's stomach what may not befall the mind when it is bent on nature's doings?

And thus it was that the gloomy Indian Jimmie Friday, despite his tuberculosis begotten of insufficient nourishment, was happy in these strange days—even to the extent of looking with wonderous eyes on the nooks which we loved—nooks which previously for him had only sheltered possible "dead-falls" or not, as the discerning eye of the trapper decided the prospects for pelf.

Going ashore on a sandy beach, Jimmie wandered down its length, his hunter mind seeking out the footprints of his prey. He stooped down, and then beckoned me to come, which I did.

Pointing at the sand, he said, "You know him?"

"Wolves," I answered.

"Yes—first time I see 'em up here—they be follerin' the deers—bad—bad. No can trap 'em—verrie smart."

A half-dozen wolves had chased a deer into the water, so they had stopped and drank, and then gone rollicking together up the beach. There were cubs, and one great track as big as a mastiff might make.

"See that—moose track—he go by yesterday;" and Jimmie pointed to enormous footprints in the muck of a marshy place. "Verrie big moose—we make call at next camp—think it is early for call."

At the next camp Jimmie made the usual birch-bark moose-call, and at evening blew it, as he also did on the following morning. This camp was a divine spot on a rise back of a long sandy beach, and we concluded to stop for a day. The Norseman and I each took a man in our canoes and started out to explore. I wanted to observe some muskrat hotels down in a big marsh, and the Norseman was fishing. The attorney was content to sit on a log by the shore of the lake, smoking lazily, and watch the sun shimmer through the lifting fog. He saw a canoe approaching from across the lake. He gazed vacantly at it, when it grew strange and more unlike a canoe. The paddles did not move, but the phantom craft drew quickly on.

"Say, Furguson—come here—look at that canoe."

The Scotsman came down, with a pail in one hand, and looked. "Canoe—hell—it's a moose—and there ain't a pocket-pistol in this camp," and he fairly jumped up and down.

"You don't say—you really don't say!" gasped the lawyer, who now began to exhibit signs of insanity.

"Yes—he's going to be damned sociable with us—he's coming right bang into this camp."

The Indian too came down, and he was long past talking English, and the gutturals came up in lumps, as though he was trying to keep them down.

The moose finally struck a long point of sand and rushes about two-hundred yards away, and drew majestically out of the water, his hide dripping, and the sun glistening on his antlers and back.

The three men gazed in spellbound admiration at the picture until the moose was gone. When they had recovered their senses they slowly went up to the camp on the ridge—disgusted and dumbfounded.

"I could almost put a cartridge in that old gun-case and kill him," sighed the backwoodsman.

"I have never hunted in my life," mused the attorney, "but few men have seen such a sight," and he filled his pipe.

"Hark—listen!" said the Indian. There was a faint cracking, which presently became louder. "He's coming into camp;" and the Indian nearly died from excitement as he grabbed a hatchet. The three unfortunate men stepped to the back of the tents, and as big a bull moose as walks came up within one hundred and fifty feet of the camp, and stopped, returning their gaze.

Thus they stood for what they say was a minute, but which seemed like hours. The attorney composedly admired the unusual sight. The Indian and Furguson swore softly but most viciously until the moose moved away. The Indian hurled the hatchet at the retreating figure with a final curse, and the thing was over.

"Those fellows who are out in their canoes will be sick abed when we tell them what's been going on in the camp this morning," sighed Mr. Furguson, as he scoured a cooking-pot.

I fear we would have had that moose on our consciences if we had been there: the game law was not up at the time, but I should have asked for strength from a higher source than my respect for law.

The golden days passed and the lake grew great. The wind blew at our backs. The waves rolled in restless surges, piling the little canoes on their crests and swallowing them in their troughs. The canoes thrashed the water as they flew along, half in, half out, but they rode like ducks. The Abwees took off their hats, gripped their double blades, made the water swirl behind them, howled in glee to each other through the rushing storm. To be five miles from shore in a seaway in kayaks like ours was a sensation. We found they stood it well, and grew contented. It was the complement to the golden lazy days when the water was glass, and the canoes rode up-side down over its mirror surface. The Norseman grinned and shook his head in token of his pleasure, much as an epicure might after a sip of superior Burgundy.

"How do you fancy this?" was asked the attorney-at-law.

"I am not going to deliver an opinion until I get ashore. I would never have believed that I would be here at my time of life, but one never knows what a fool one can make of one's self. My glasses are covered with water, and I can hardly see, but I can't let go of this paddle to wipe them," shrieked the man of the office chair, in the howl of the weather.

But we made a long journey by the aid of the wind, and grew a contempt for it. How could one imagine the stability of those little boats until one had tried it?

That night we put into a natural harbor and camped on a gravel beach. The tents were up and the supper cooking, when the wind hauled and blew furiously into our haven. The fires were scattered and the rain came in blinding sheets. The tent-pegs pulled from the sand. We sprang to our feet and held on to the poles, wet to the skin. It was useless; the rain blew right under the canvas. We laid the tents on the "grub" and stepped out into the dark. We could not be any wetter, and we did not care. To stand in the dark in the wilderness, with nothing to eat, and a fire-engine playing a hose on you for a couple of hours—if you have imagination enough, you can fill in the situation. But the gods were propitious. The wind died down. The stars came out by myriads. The fires were relighted, and the ordinary life begun. It was late in the night before our clothes, blankets, and tents were dry, but, like boys, we forgot it all.

Then came a river—blue and flat like the sky above—running through rushy banks, backed by the masses of the forest; anon the waters rushed upon us over the rocks, and we fought, plunk-plunk-plunk, with the paddles, until our strength gave out. We stepped out into the water, and getting our lines, and using our long double blades as fenders, "tracked" the canoes up through the boil. The Indians in their heavier boats used "setting-poles" with marvelous dexterity, and by furious exertion were able to draw steadily up the grade—though at times they too "tracked," and even portaged. Our largest canoe weighed two hundred pounds, but a little voyager managed to lug it, though how I can't comprehend, since his pipestem legs fairly bent and wobbled under the enormous ark. None of us by this time were able to lift the loads which we carried, but, like a Western pack-mule, we stood about and had things piled on to us, until nothing more would stick. Some of the backwoodsmen carry incredible masses of stuff, and their lore is full of tales which no one could be expected to believe. Our men did not hesitate to take two hundred and fifty pounds over short portages, which were very rough and stony, though they all said if they slipped they expected to break a leg. This is largely due to the tump-line, which is laid over the head, while persons unused to it must have shoulder-straps in addition, which are not as good, because the "breastbone," so called, is not strong enough.

We were getting day by day farther into "the beyond." There were no traces here of the hand of man. Only Jimmie knew the way—it was his trapping ground. Only once did we encounter people. We were blown into a little board dock, on a gray day, with the waves piling up behind us, and made a difficult landing. Here were a few tiny log houses—an outpost of the Hudson Bay Company. We renewed our stock of provisions, after laborious trading with the stagnated people who live in the lonely place. There was nothing to sell us but a few of the most common necessities; however, we needed only potatoes and sugar. This was Jimmie's home. Here we saw his poor old mother, who was being tossed about in the smallest of canoes as she drew her nets. Jimmie's father had gone on a hunting expedition and had never come back. Some day Jimmie's old mother will go out on the wild lake to tend her nets, and she will not come back. Some time Jimmie too will not return—for this Indian struggle with nature is appalling in its fierceness.

There was a dance at the post, which the boys attended, going by canoe at night, and they came back early in the morning, with much giggling at their gallantries.

The loneliness of this forest life is positively discouraging to think about. What the long winters must be in the little cabins I cannot imagine, and I fear the traders must be all avarice, or have none at all; for there can certainly be no intellectual life. There is undoubtedly work, but not one single problem concerning it. The Indian hunters do fairly well financially, though their lives are beset with weakening hardships and constant danger. Their meagre diet wears out their constitutions, and they are subject to disease. The simplicity of their minds make it very difficult to see into their life as they try to narrate it to one who may be interested.

From here on was through beautiful little lakes, and the voyagers rigged blanket sails on the big canoes, while we towed behind. Then came the river and the rapids, which we ran, darting between rocks, bumping on sunken stones—shooting fairly out into the open air, all but turning over hundreds of times. One day the Abwees glided out in the big lake Tesmiaquemang, and saw the steamer going to Bais des Pierres. We hailed her, and she stopped, while the little canoes danced about in the swell as we were loaded one by one. On the deck above us the passengers admired a kind of boat the like of which had not before appeared in these parts.

At Bais des Pierres we handed over the residue of the commissaries of the Abwee-Chemun to Jimmie Friday, including personally many pairs of well worn golf-breeches, sweaters, rubber coats, knives which would be prescribed by law in New York. If Jimmie ever parades his solemn wilderness in these garbs, the owls will laugh from the trees. Our simple forest friend laid in his winter stock—traps, flour, salt, tobacco, and pork, a new axe—and accompanied us back down the lake again on the steamer. She stopped in mid-stream, while Jimmie got his bundles into his "bark" and shoved off, amid a hail of "good-byes."

The engine palpitated, the big wheel churned the water astern, and we drew away. Jimmie bent on his paddle with the quick body-swing habitual to the Indian, and after a time grew a speck on the reflection of the red sunset in Temiscamingue.

The Abwees sat sadly leaning on the after-rail, and agreed that Jimmie was "a lovely Injun." Jimmie had gone into the shade of the overhang of the cliffs, when the Norseman started violently up; put his hands in his pockets, stamped his foot, said, "By George, fellows, any D. F. would call this a sporting trip!" ■ ■

TOO BIG GAME FOR NUMBER SIX

The Blue Quail of the Cactus

This story first appeared in Harper's *New Monthly Magazine*, October 1896 and later in *Crooked Trails*.

THE QUARTERMASTER AND I both had trouble which the doctors could not cure—it was January, and it would not do for us to sit in a blind; besides, I do not fancy that. There are ever so many men who are comfortable all over when they are sitting in a blind waiting on the vagrant flying of the ducks; but it is solemn, gloomy business, and I must say, sufficient reason why they take a drink every fifteen minutes to keep up their enthusiasm. We both knew that the finest winter resort for shot-gun folks was in the Southwest—down on the Rio Grande in Texas— so we journeyed to Eagle Pass. As we got down from the train we saw Captain Febiger in his long military cloak by a lantern-light.

"Got any quail staked out for us, Feb?" asked the Quartermaster.

"Oodles," said Febiger; "get into my trap," and we were rattled through the streets out to the camp, and brought up by the Captain's quarters.

In the morning we unpacked our trunks, and had everything on the floor where we could see it, after the fashion with men. Captain Febiger's baby boy came in to help us rummage in the heaps of canvas clothes, ammunition, and what not besides, finally selecting for his amusement a loaded Colt's revolver and a freshly honed razor. We were terrorized by the pos-

131

sibilities of the combination. Our trying to take them away from the youngster only made him yell like a cavern of demons. We howled for his mother to come to our aid, which she finally did, and she separated the kid from his toys.

I put on my bloomers, when the Captain came in and viewed me, saying: "Texas bikes; but it doesn't bloom yet. I just don't know what Texas will do if you parade in those togs—but you can try."

As we sauntered down the dusty main street, Texas lounged in the doorways or stood up in its buggy and stared at me. Texas grinned cheerfully, too, but I did not care, so long as Texas kept its hand out of its hip pocket. I was content to help educate Texas as to personal comfort, at no matter what cost to myself. We passed into Mexico over the Long Bridge to call on Senor Munos, who is the local czar, in hopes of getting permits to be let alone by his chaparral-rangers while we shot quail on their soil. In Mexico when the people observe an Americano they simply shrug their shoulders; so our bloomers attracted no more contempt than would an X-ray or a trolley car. Senor Munos gave the permits, after much stately compliments and many subtle ways, which made us feel under a cloud of obligation.

The next morning an ambulance and escort-wagon drove up to the Captain's quarters, and we loaded ourselves in—shot-guns, ammunition, blankets, and the precious paper of Senor Munos; for, only the week before, the custom-house runners had carefully escorted an American hunting party a long distance back to the line for lack of the little paper and red seals. We rattled over the bridge, past the Mexican barrack, while its dark-skinned soldiery—who do not shoot quails—lounged in the sunshine against the whitewashed wall.

At the first outpost of the customs a little man, whose considerable equatorial proportions were girted with a gun, examined our paper, and waved us on our way. Under the railroad bridge of the International an engineer blew his whistle, and our mules climbed on top of each other in their terror. We wound along the little river, through irrigating ditches, past dozens of those deliciously quaint adobe houses, past the inevitable church, past a dead pony, ran over a chicken, made the little seven-year-old girls take their five-year-old brothers up in their arms for protection, and finally we climbed a long hill. At the top stretched an endless plain. The road forked; presently it branched; anon it grew into twigs of white dust on the gray levels of the background. The local physician of Eagle Pass was of our party, and he was said to know where a certain tank was to be found, some thirty miles out in the desert, but no man yet created could know which twig of the road to take. He decided on one—changed his mind—got out of the ambulance, scratched his head, pondered, and finally resolution settled on his face. He motioned the driver to a certain twig, got in, and shut his mouth firmly, thus closing debate. We smoked silently, waiting for the doctor's mind to fog. He turned uneasily in his seat, like the agitated needle of a compass, and even in time hazarded the remark that something did not look natural; but there was nothing to look at but flat land and flat sky, unless a hawk sailing here or there. At noon we lunched at the tail of the ambulance, and gently "jollied" the doctor's topography. We pushed on. Later in the afternoon the thirsty mules went slowly. The doctor had by this time admitted his doubts—some long blue hills on the sky-line ought to be further to the west, according to his remembrance. As no one else had any ideas on the subject, the doctor's position was not enviable. We changed our course, and traveled many weary miles through the chaparral, which was high enough to stop our vision, and stiff enough to bar our way, keeping us to narrow roads. At last the bisecting cattle trails began to converge, and we knew that they lead to water—which they did; for shortly we saw a little broken adobe, a tumbled brush corral, the plastered gate of an acequia, and the blue water of the tank.

To give everything its due proportion at this point, we gathered to congratulate the doctor as we passed the flask. The camp was pitched within the corral, and while the cook got supper, we stood in the after-glow on the bank of the tank and saw the ducks come home, heard the mud-hens squaddle, while high in the air flew the long line of sand-hill cranes with a hoarse clangor. It was quite dark when we sat on the "grub" chests and ate by the firelight, while out in the desert the coyotes shrilled to the monotonous accompaniment of the mules crunching their feed and stamping wearily. Tomorrow it was proposed to hunt ducks in their flight, which means getting up before daylight, so bed found us early. It seemed but a minute after I had sought my blankets when I was being abused by the Captain, being pushed with his foot—fairly rolled over by him—he even standing on my body as he shouted: "Get up, if you are going to hunt. It will be light directly—get up!" And this, constantly recurring, is one reason why I do not care for duck-shooting.

But, in order to hunt, I had to get up, and file off in the line of ghosts, stumbling, catching on the chaparral, and splashing in the mud. I led a setter-dog, and was presently directed to sit down in some damp grass, because it was a good place—certainly not to sit down in, but for other reasons. I sat there in the dark, petting the good dog, and watching it grow pale in the east. This is not to mention the desire for breakfast, or the damp, or the sleepiness, but this is really the larger part of duck-hunting. Of course if I later had a dozen good shots it might compensate—but I did not have a dozen shots.

The day came slowly out of the east, the mud-hens came out of the marsh splashing about in the rushes, a sailing hawk was visible against the gray sky overhead, and I felt rather insignificant, not to say contemptible,

LUNCHEON IN THE DESERT

134

as I sat there in the loneliness of this big nature which worked around me. The dog dignified the situation—he was a part of nature's belongings—while I somehow did not seem to grace the solitude. The grays slowly grew into browns on the sedge-grass, and the water to silver. A bright flash of fire shot out of the dusk far up in the gloom, and the dull report of a shot-gun came over the tank. Black objects flew across the sky—the ducks were flying. I missed one or two, and grew weary—none came near enough to my lair. Presently it was light, and I got a fair shot. My bird tumbled into the rushes out in front of me, and the setter bounded in to retrieve. He searched vehemently, but the wounded duck dived in front of him, he came ashore shortly, and lying down, he bit at himself and pawed and rolled. He was a mass of cockle-burs. I took him on my lap and laboriously picked them out of his hair for a half-hour; then, shouldering my gun I turned tragically to the water and anathematized its ducks—all ducks, my fellow-duckers, all thoughts and motives concerning ducks—and then strode into the chaparral.

"Hie on! hie on!" I tossed my arm, and the setter began to hunt beautifully—glad, no doubt, to leave all thoughts of the cockle-burs and evasive ducks behind. I worked up the shore of the tank, keeping back in the brush, and got some fun. After chasing about for some time I came out near the water. My dog pointed. I glided forward, and came near shooting the Quartermaster, who sat in a bunch of sedge-grass, with a dead duck by his side. He was smoking, and disgusted with ducks. He joined me, and shortly, as we crossed the road, the long Texas doctor, who owned the dog, came striding down the way. He was ready for quail now, and we started.

This quail hunting is active work. The dog points, but one nearly always finds the birds running from one prickly-pear bush to another. They do not stand, rarely flush, and when they do get up it is only to swoop ahead to the nearest cover, where they settle quickly. One must be sharp in his shooting—he cannot select his distance, for the cactus lies thick about, and the little running bird is only on view for the shortest of moments. You must overrun a dog after his first point, since he works too close behind them. The covey will keep together if not pursued with too much haste, and one gets shot after shot; still, at last you must run lively, as the frightened covey scurry along at a lively pace. Heavy shot are necessary, since the blue quail carry lead like Marshal Massena, and are much harder to kill than the bob-white. Three men working together can get shooting enough out of a bunch—the chase often continuing for a mile, when the covey gradually separate, the sportsmen following separate birds.

Where the prickly-pear cactus is thickest, there are the blue quail, since that is their feed and water supply. This same cactus makes a difficulty of pursuit, for it bristles with spines, which come off on your clothing, and when they enter the skin make most uncomfortable and persistent sores. The Quartermaster had an Indian tobacco-bag dangling at his belt, and as it flopped in his progress it gathered prickers which it shortly transferred to his luckless legs, until he at last detected the reason why he bristled so fiercely. And the poor dog—at every covey we had to stop and pick needles out of him. The haunts of the blue quail are really no place for a dog, as he soon becomes useless. One does not need him, either, since the blue quail will not flush until actually kicked into the air.

Jack and cotton-tail rabbits fled by hundreds before us. They are everywhere, and afford good shooting between coveys, it being quick work to get a cotton-tail as he flashes between the network of protecting cactus. Coyotes lope away in our front, but they are too wild for a shot-gun. It must ever be in man's mind to keep his direction, because it is such a vastly simple thing to get lost in the chaparral, where you cannot see a hundred yards. Mexico is such a considerable territory that a man on foot may find it inconvenient to beat up a town in the desolation of thorn-bush.

There is an action about blue quail shooting which is next to buffalo shooting—it's run, shoot, pick up your bird, scramble on in your endeavor to keep the skirmish-line of your two comrades; and at last, when you have concluded to stop, you can mop your forehead—the Mexican sun shines hot even in midwinter.

Later in the afternoon we get among bob-white in a grassy tract, and while they are clean work—good dog play, and altogether more satisfactory shooting than any other I know of—I am yet much inclined to the excitement of chasing after game which you can see at intervals. Let it not be supposed that it is less difficult to hit a running blue quail as he shoots through the brush than a flying bob-white, for the experience of our party has settled that, and one gets ten shots at the blue to one at the bob-white, because of their number. As to eating, we could not tell the difference; but I will not insist that this is final. A man who comes in from an all day's run in the brush does not care whether the cook gives him boiled beans, watermelon, or crackers and jam; so how is he to know what a bird's taste is when served to a tame appetite?

At intervals we ran into the wild cattle which threaded their way to water, and it makes one nervous. It is of no use to say "Soo-bossy," or to give him a charge of No. 6; neither is it well to run. If the matadores had any of the sensations which I have experienced, the gate receipts at the bull-rings would have to go up. When a big long-horn fastens a quail-shooter with his great open brown eye in a chaparral thicket, you are not inclined to "call his hand." If he will call it a misdeal, you are with him.

We were banging away, the Quartermaster and I, when a human

ON THE SHORE OF THE TANK

voice began yelling like mad from the brush ahead. We advanced, to find a Mexican—rather well gotten up—who proceeded to wave his arms like a parson who had reached "sixthly" in his sermon, and who proceeded thereat to overwhelm us with his eloquence. The Quartermaster and I "buenos dias-ed" and "si, senor-ed" him in our helpless Spanish, and asked each other, nervously, "What de'll." After a long time he seemed to be getting through with his subject, his sentences became separated, he finally emitted monosyllables only along with his scowls, and we tramped off into the brush. It was a pity he spent so much energy, since it could only arouse our curiosity without satisfying it.

In camp that night we told the Captain of the excited Mexican friend out in the brush, and our cook had seen sinister men on ponies passing near the camp. The Captain became solicitous, and stationed a night-guard over his precious government mules. It would never do to have a bandit get away with a U. S. brand. It never does matter about private property, but anything with U. S. on it has got to be looked after, like a croupy child.

We had some good days' sport, and no more formidable enterprise against the night-guard was attempted than the noisy approach of a white jack-ass. The tents were struck and loaded when it began to rain. We stood in the shelter of the escort-wagon, and the storm rose to a hurricane. Our corral became a tank; but shortly the black clouds passed north, and we pulled out. The twig ran into a branch, and the branch struck the trunk near the bluffs over the Rio Grande, and in town there stood the Mexican soldiers leaning against the wall as we had left them. We wondered if they had moved meanwhile. ■ ■

137

NOON-DAY TEA

138

The White Forest

"The White Forest" first appeared in Harper's *New Monthly Magazine*, December 1898. It later became a part of Remington's book, *Men with the Bark On*.

FROM THE MID-WINTER MIST and mush of New York it was a transformation to us standing there in the smoking-room of the Chateau Frontenac at Quebec, looking down across the grand reaches of the St. Lawrence, where the ice ran in crashing fields through the steaming water of the flood-tide. It was a cheerful view, though the frost was on the pane, and the wood-work popped with the cold. Down in the street the little Canadian horses, drawing their loads, were white with rime, while their irrepressible French drivers yelled at each other until we could hear them through the double windows. There is energy in this fierce northern air.

"Why Florida in winter? Why not Quebec?" said the old Yale stroke.

"Yes, why not?" reiterated the Essex trooper.

But the coziness of the chateau did not suggest the seriousness of our purpose. We wanted to get out on the snow—to get in the snow—to tempt its moods and feel its impulses. We wanted to feel the nip of that keen outside air, to challenge a contest with our woolens, and to appropriate some of its energy. Accordingly we consulted a wise mind who sold snow-shoes, blankets, moccasins, and socks, and he did a good business.

"Shall we dress at St. Raymond or in the chateau?" said my companion, mindful of the severity of convention in New York, as he gazed on the litter of his new garments spread out on the floor of our room.

"We will dress here, and leave so early that Quebec will not be out of bed until we are away; but if Quebec were awake and on the streets, Quebec would not turn its head to honor our strangeness with a glance, because it would see nothing new in us;" and dress we did. We only put on three pairs of socks and one pair of flannel-lined moccasins, but we were taught later to put on all we had. As the rich man said to the reporter, when trying to explain the magnitude of his coming ball, "There will be ten thousand dollars' worth of ice-cream," so I say to you we had forty dollars' worth of yarn socks.

We had bags of blankets, hunks of fresh beef and pork, which had to be thawed for hours before cooking, and potatoes in a gunny sack, which rattled like billiard-balls, so hard were they frozen. We found great amusement on the train by rattling the bag of potatoes, for they were the hardest, the most dense things known to science.

The French drivers of the burleaus who deposited us at the train took a cheery interest in our affairs; they lashed the horses, yelled like fiends, made the snow fly around the corners, nearly ran down an early policeman, and made us happy with the animation. They are rough children, amazingly polite—a product of paternalism—and comfortable folks to have around, only you must be careful not to let them succeed in their childish endeavor to drive their horses over you. Anyway, they cheered us off through the softly falling snow of that early winter morning, and made us feel less like strangers.

At St. Raymond were the guides and little one-horse burleaus all ready for the trip to the "bush," or at least for the fifteen miles, which is as far as sleighs could go, up to old man O'Shannahan's, which is the first camp of the club. There were nearly four feet of snow on the ground, so that the regular road between the fences was drifted full, compelling the habitants to mark out another way with evergreen trees through their fields.

Far apart over the white landscape are set the little French cottages, with their curved roofs. They are so cozily lonely, and the rough hills go up from the valley to further isolate them. Coming along the road we met the low hauling-sleds of the natives, who ran their horses off the road into the snow half-way up their horses' sides; but the sledges were flat, and floated, as it were. Picturesque fellows, with tuques, red sashes, and fur coats, and whiskers worn under their chin, after the fashion of the early thirties. The Quebec habitants don't bother their heads about the new things, which is the great reason why they are the most contented people in America.

The faithful watch-dog barked at us from every cottage, and, after the manner of all honest house-dogs, charged us, with skinned lips and gleaming eye. We waited until they came near to the low-set burleau, when we menaced them with the whip, whereat they sprang from the hard road into the soft snow, going out of sight in it, where their floundering made us laugh loud and long. Dogs do not like to be laughed at, and it is so seldom one gets even with the way-side pup.

At O'Shannahan's we were put up in the little club cabin and made comfortable. I liked everything in the country except the rough look of the hills, knowing, as I do, that all the game in America has in these latter days been forced into them, and realizing that to follow it the hunter must elevate himself over the highest tops, which process never became mixed in my mind with the poetry of mountain scenery.

We essayed the snow-shoes—an art neglected by us three people since our boyhood days. It is like horseback-riding—one must be at it all the time if he is to feel comfortable. Snow-shoes must be understood, or they will not get along with you.

Bebe Larette laughingly said, "Purty soon you mak de snow shoe go more less lak dey was crazee."

Having arranged to haul the supplies into the "bush" next day, we lay down for the night in the warm cabin, tucked in and babied by our generous French guides. The good old Irishman, Mr. O'Shannahan, was the last to withdraw.

"Mr. O'Shannahan, what do the French say for 'good-night'?"

"Well, som' o' thim says 'Bung way'; but none of them, I imagine, say it just like Mr. O'Shannahan."

With the daylight our hut began to abound with the activities of the coming day. A guide had a fire going, and Mr. O'Shannahan stood warming himself beside it. The Essex trooper, having reduced himself to the buff, put on an old pair of moccasins and walked out into the snow. The New Jersey thermometer which we had brought along may not have as yet gotten acclimated, but it solemnly registered 5° below zero.

"Bebe, will you kindly throw a bucket of water over my back?" he asked; but Bebe might as well have been asked to kindly shoot the Essex trooper with a gun, or to hit him with an axe. Bebe would have neither ice-water, rifle, nor axe on his pious soul.

I know the stern requirements of the morning bath, and doused him with the desired water, when he capered into the cabin and began with his crash towel to rub for the reaction. Seeing that Mr. O'Shannahan was perturbed, I said,

"What do you think of that act?"

"Oi think a mon is ez will aff be the soide av this stove as to be havin' the loikes av yez poor ice-wather down his spoine."

Mr. O'Shannahan reflected and hunched nearer the box-stove, saying: "It's now gone a year, but oi did say a mon do mooch the loikes av that wan day. He divisted himself av his last stitch, an' dayliberately wint out an' rowled himsilf in the snow. That before brikfast, moind ye. Oi've no doobt he's long since dead. Av the loikes av this t'ing do be goan an, an' is rayparted down en the Parlamint, they'll be havin' a law fer it—more's the nade."

After breakfast a hundred pounds of our war material was loaded on each toboggan. We girded on our snow-shoes and started out to break trail for the sledges. I know of no more arduous work. And while the weather was very cold, Mr. O'Shannahan nearly undressed us before he was satisfied at our condition for bush-ranging. We sank from eight to ten inches in the soft snow. The raising of the snow-burdened racket tells on lung and ankle and loin with killing force. Like everything else, one might become accustomed to lugging say ten pounds extra on each set of toes, but he would have to take more than a day at it. The perspiration comes in streams, which showed the good of O'Shannahan's judgment. Besides, before we had gone three miles we began to understand the mistake of not wearing our forty dollars' worth of socks. Also we had our moccasins on the outside, or next to the snowshoes. They got damp, froze into something like sheet-iron, and had a fine glaze on their bottoms, which made them slip and slide backward and forward on the snow-shoes.

After three miles, Bebe readjusted and tied my moccasins, when Oliver, the cook, who was a very intelligent man, mopped his forehead with his shirt sleeve, and observed:

"Excuse me, I t'ink you bettair go back dose cabain—you are not fix hup more propair for dees beesness. Ma dear fren', dose man een Quebec what sol' you dose t'ing"—and here his quiet, patient personality was almost overcome, this human reflection of the long Northern winter could not calm himself, so he blurted, in his peaceful way—"dose man een Quebec dey weare no not'ing."

We were in the light of a great truth—the shoes would not stay on— the thongs cut our toes—we had outlived our usefulness as trail-breakers, and we succumbed. The back track was one of my greatest misfortunes in life, but it was such a measly lot of cold-finger, frozen-toe, slip-down detail that I will forbear. My companions were equally unfortunate; so when we finally fell into the arms of Mr. O'Shannahan, he said:

"Ah, a great hardship. Oi will make that matter plain to yez."

The sledges had deposited their loads half-way up the trail, the guides coming back for the night.

Next morning the remainder of our stuff was loaded, and with renewed faith we strode forth. The snow-shoes were now all right, and, with five pairs of socks apiece—one outside the moccasins—the thongs could not eat our toes. We took photographs of our moccasins—unwholesome, swollen things—and dedicated the plates to Mr. Kipling as "the feet of the young men."

The country of the Little Saguenay is as rough as any part of the Rocky Mountains. It is the custom to dress lightly for traveling, notwithstanding the 20° below zero, and even when one perspires very freely, making it impossible to stop for a rest, on account of the chill of the open pores. Ice forms on eyebrow, hair, and mustache, while the sweat freezes in scales on the back of one's neck. The snow falls from the trees on the voyager, and melting slightly from the heat of the body, forms cakes of ice. Shades of Nansen and all the arctic men! I do not understand why they are not all pillars of ice, unless it be that there are no trees to dump snow on them. The spruce and hemlock of these parts all point upward as straight as one could set a lance, to resist the constant fall of snow. If one leaned out ever so little from the perpendicular, it could not survive the tremendous average of fifty feet of snowfall each winter. Their branches, too, do not grow long, else they would snap under the weight. Every needle on the evergreens had its little burden of white,

THE WHITE FOREST

and without intermission the snow comes sifting down from the sky through the hush of the winter. When we stopped, and the creak of the snow-shoes was still, we could almost hear our hearts beat. We could certainly hear the cracking of the tobacco burning in our pipes. It had a soothing, an almost seductive influence, that muffle of snow. So solemn is it, so little you feel yourself, that it is a consciousness which brings unconsciousness, and the calm white forest is almost deadening in its beauty. The winter forest means death.

Then came the guides dragging their tobbogans, and we could hear them pant and grunt and creak and slip; how they manage the fearful work is quite beyond me. Used to it I suppose. So are pack-mules; but think of the generations of suffering behind this which alone makes it possible. The men of the pack, the paddle, snow-shoe, toboggan, and axe do harder, more exhausting work than any other set of people; they are nearer to the primitive strain against the world of matter than are other men—they are the "wheelers," so to speak.

The last stage up the mountain was a lung-burster, but finally we got to the lake, which was our objective. It was smooth.

"Let us take off these instruments of torture and rest our feet on the smooth going," said we, in our innocence, and we undid a snow-shoe each. The released foot went into the snow up to our middles, and into water besides. We resumed our snow-shoe, but the wet moccasins coming in contact with the chill air became as iron. Our frozen snow-shoe thongs were wires of steel. Our hands were cold with the work of readjustment, our bodies chilled with the waiting. It was a bad half-hour before the cabin was reached. We built a fire, but the provisions had not come up, so we sat around and gazed with glaring eye at each other. The Essex trooper talked of eating the old Yale stroke, who was our companion, but we agreed he was too tough. I was afraid for a time that a combination might be made against me on those lines, but luckily the toboggans arrived.

The log cabin was seventeen feet square, so what with the room taken by the bunks, box-stove, our provender and dunnage, the lobby of the house was somewhat crowded. There were three Americans and five Frenchmen. The stove was of the most excitable kind, never satisfied to do its mere duty, but threatening a holocaust with every fresh stick of wood. We made what we called "atmospheric cocktails" by opening the door and letting in one part of 20° below zero air to two parts of 165° above zero air, seasoned with French bitters. It had the usual effect of all cocktails; we should much have preferred the "straight goods" at, say, 70°.

In the morning we began a week's work at caribou-hunting. It is proper to state at this interval that this article can have no "third act," for success did not crown our efforts. We scoured the woods industriously behind our India-rubber, leather-lunged guides, with their expert snow-shoeing, and saw many caribou; but they saw us first, or smelled us, or

HUNTING THE CARIBOU—"SHOOT! SHOOT!"

heard us, and, with the exception of two "clean misses," we had no chance. It may be of interest to tell what befalls those who "miss," according to the rough law of the cabin. The returning hunter may deny it vigorously, but the grinning of the guide is ample testimony for conviction. The hunter is led to the torture tree. All the men, cook included, pour out of the cabin and line up. The "misser" is required to assume a very undignified posture, when all the men take a hack at him with a frozen moccasin. It is rude fun, but the howls of laughter ring through the still forest, and even the unfortunate sportsman feels that he has atoned for his deed.

Bebe Larette killed a young caribou, which was brought into camp for our observation. It was of a color different from what we had expected, darker on the back, blacker on the muzzle, and more the color of the tree trunks among which it lives. Indeed, we had it frozen and set up in the timber to be photographed and painted. Standing there, it was almost invisible in its sameness.

Its feet were the chief interest, for we had all seen and examined its tracks. If one puts his hand down inside the track, he will find a hard pillar of snow which is compressed by their cuplike feet; and more striking still is it that the caribou does not sink in the snow as far as our big

145

THE HOT FINISH IN THE SNOW SHOE RACE

snow-shoes, not even when it runs, which it is able to do in four feet of snow with the speed of a red deer on dry ground. In these parts the caribou has no enemy but man: the wolf and the panther do not live here, though the lynx does, but I could not learn that he attacks the caribou.

For sportsmen who hunt in the fall of the year he is not regarded as especially difficult. He is easily shot from boats around ponds; but to kill a caribou in the Laurentian Mountains in midwinter is indeed a feat. This is due to the deathly stillness of the winter forest, and the snow-shoeing difficulties which beset even the most clever sportsman.

This brings to my mind the observation that snow-shoeing, as a hunter is required to do it when on the caribou track, has the same relationship to the "club snow-shoe run," so called, that "park riding" does to "punching cows." The men of the bush have short and oval shoes, and they must go up and down the steepest imaginable places, and pass at good speed and perfect silence through the most dense spruce and tamarack thickets, for there the caribou leads. The deep snow covers up the small evergreen bushes, but they resist it somewhat, leaving a soft spot, which the hunter is constantly falling into with fatal noise. If he runs against a tree, down comes an avalanche of snow, which sounds like thunder in the quiet.

I was brought to a perfectly fresh track of three caribou by two guides, and taking the trail, we found them not alarmed, but traveling rapidly. So hot was the trail that I removed the stocking from my gun breech. We moved on with as much speed as we could manage in silence.

146

The trees were cones of snow, making the forest dense, like soft-wood timber in summer. We were led up hills, through dense hemlock thickets, where the falling snow nearly clogged the action of my rifle and filled the sights with ice. I was forced to remove my right mitten to keep them ice-clear by warming with the bare hand. The snow-shoeing was difficult and fatiguing to the utmost, as mile after mile we wound along after those vagrant caribou. We found a small pond where they had pawed for water, and it had not yet frozen from their drink.

Now is the time when the hunter feels the thrill which is the pleasure of the sport.

Down the sides of the pond led the trail, then twisting and turning, it entered the woods and wound up a little hill. Old man Larette fumbled the snow with his bare hand; he lifted toward us some unfrozen spoor— good, cheerful old soul, his eyes were those of a panther. Now we set our shoes ever so carefully, pressed them down slowly, and shifted our weight cautiously lest the footing be false. The two hunters crouched in the snow, pointing. I cocked my rifle; one snow-shoe sank slowly under me—the snow was treacherous—and three dark objects flitted like birds past the only opening in the forest, seventy-five yards ahead.

"Take the gun, Con," I said, and my voice broke on the stillness harshly: the game was up, the disappointment keen. The reaction of disgust was equal to the suppressed elation of the second before.

The country was full of caribou. They travel constantly, not staying in one section. New tracks came every day into our little territory. We stalked and worked until our patience gave out, when we again loaded our toboggans for the back track.

At Mr. O'Shannahan's we got our burleaus, and jingled into St. Raymond by the light of the moon. ■ ■

MAKING THE SNOW SHOE

TROUT FISHING IN CANADA

How a Trout Broke a Friendship

The appearance of Remington's short story "How A Trout Broke A Friendship" in *Outing*, September 1900 was not accompanied by the usual illustrations. There did appear in *Collier's Weekly*, dated August 3, 1901, a full page plate entitled "Trout Fishing in Canada." This illustration seemed so typical of the story that it is here reproduced in conjunction with it. The painting was also reproduced in Remington's *Done In The Open* published by R. H. Russell, New York, 1902.

I F I WERE AN ANGLER there would be no story, but I shall wish all my days that I had been a fisherman when I think of how my lack of experience refrigerated the nature of my old friend Joel.

It was early spring in Canada, and Lake Edwards was ice-water. I was camped on a point of rocks in company with three "complete anglers" and three French Indians. A chilling rain had fallen incessantly for days; the fish would not be suited by any fly in our books. Everything was soggy and mildewed. An ill-tempered little box-stove smoldered but helped to keep our miserable bodies alive. Our minds were becoming jaded by a draw-poker game which seemed to have had no beginning. As I view the situation from afar, I can perceive how carefully tilled was that ground to bear the seeds of trouble.

They were all friends of mine, with strong mutual sympathies in many directions; but they were fishermen, while I was not. They were men who at home have sacred dens in their houses, and in them they worship a heathen god in the form of a glass case full of dainty rods. They have hundreds of flies suited to all kinds of moods of all kinds of fish. They have stuffed bass and wadded trout, colored artificially as falsely as a rose on Indian trade calico. There are creels, reels, silver ammunition flasks, rare prints of the forefathers of the lure, books of tall stories so dear to the craft, and things which you and I could not call by name.

In such places these men gather—through the tobacco smoke the lakes blow softly, the ponds wait idly and the brooks bubble pleasantly in imagination.

These fellows mix fish up with their dessert and coffee, and in importance to them old Leonard is to President McKinley as a million to one.

So things to fish with to these men, things of wood, and silk, and steel, are vested with souls almost. They are like Japanese jugs or early English portraits to other enthusiasts.

The trout of Lake Edward floated idly beneath the boats, and if they looked at our bait they did no more, in consequence of which the anglers sat on boxes and dealt five cards round on the top of a trunk, and stub-flushes took the place of "cockie-bondhus" and "Yellow-sallies."

Having been ruined by the last jack-pot, I got up and trod forth into the rain, which was beating the lake into silver. I was listless—tired of the eternal three card draw—tired of the rain and dreaming of elsewhere. I sauntered down toward the water and passed a shed under which were hung a great number of rods, all strung with reels, lines and flies.

"Why not fish—we came here to do that—that was our theory?" Suiting the action to the thought, I took down a rod at random, called a Frenchman and got into a boat.

We two sat there, the guide holding us a short way from the point of rocks. The rain poured in jumping drops on the flat water, while the pine forests faded softly into its obscuring sheets.

Presently one of our party, a gentleman from Pennsylvania, who must have encountered a disappointing jack-pot, emerged from the tent, and, calling a guide, began to cast from a boat not far away.

The poker game evidently languished, since the capitalists came out in the rain and gazed about in a yawning way. They eyed Mr. Pennsylvania and me, who am no fisherman. Then they espied a birch canoe which was one of the quickest boats I ever saw. They remembered having recently seen an Indian stand upright in the tottlish craft—a balancing feat which was the inherited trait of ages of canoe-living ancestors. This inspired a five dollar sporting proposition that one of them could do what the Indian had done. He pushed out in the canoe while my friend Joel stood on the rocks amusing himself with the thought of the easy five dollars.

At this point my rod doubled into something like a figure eight then it acted like a whip-snake having a fit—it was near to parting from me at times—the reel sang and the line hissed about in the water. The Frenchman stood up in the boat and poured Lake St. John French into me in a Maxim rumble. While this was at its height Mr. Pennsylvania hooked the mate to my whale, but he knew his business. There was a great splash in front of me, and I only glanced long enough to see that Joel had won his bet.

He tipped backward and forward, laughing until the forest echoed with his roars. Things were all his way.

The swimmer tried to board Mr. Pennsylvania's boat but was told to get away—not to bother his fish—that human life was nothing now—to swim to the rocks—don't be a damn fool.

The Cannuck French of my guide was beginning to tell on me. I was almost ready to let the fish go while I threw the Frenchman overboard. I was so hot at him that I grew cooler toward the fish end of my troubles and no doubt was doing better reel work for it all.

Events having slowed down a bit Joel began to observe things more closely. As he ran his eyes curiously over the activities on the water, they alighted on my rod. He gazed hard, earnestly, knowingly, at it. It was now in a figure eight, now bent this way now that, being half under water, and Joel raised both hands high above his head while he yelled, "You have got my rod, my seventy-five dollar Leonard rod! Cut that line! What in hell do you mean by taking my best rod?"

The editor will not let me tell you all that Joel vouchsafed on this galling occasion.

Now my affrighted friend walked the rocks like Mr. Leslie Carter in the third act of Zaza. He nearly turned handsprings, he gesticulated and roared for a boat or a deadly weapon. Steadily through it all surged his quick-chosen words of rebuke to me.

I now regretted the whole thing, but I couldn't let go and the fish wouldn't. The seventy-five dollar bamboo was getting action for the money and the Frenchman knew that war had been declared.

Seeing that his present method would never get the rod ashore without the fish, Joel changed his scheme quickly, as an able tactician should. He stood still and, beating like the leader of an orchestra, he said, "Reel him in—slowly, now—slowly, slowly. There—let him out—don't hold that rod against your belly."

There were tears streaming from the rod-owner's eyes which rivaled the rain.

"Can't you check him easily—there now! Do you think you have got a bean pole, easy, don't get excited! Baptiste, back that boat ashore."

"If you back this boat ashore I'll murder you! By George, I'll burn you alive, Baptiste!" I shouted, and nothing was done.

Joel coached, more carefully now—more intelligently—and my divided interest in the trout cooled me down until, under able direction, I finally landed a five-pound trout on the rocks, and I was no fisherman. It was one of the mistakes of my life.

Joel took his rod amid my apologies. He cared not for the latter. It was that the clumsy hands of a bean-pole, worm baiting, grill yanking outcast had taken the soul out of Leonard's masterpiece.

No longer would that rod look out to him from the middle of the glass case, seeming to say, "Your hands and my subtle curves—what, master—what can we not do?"

He sat around the tent and cast wolfish glances at me, and public sentiment sat stolidly by him. I carried an open jack-knife in my outside coat pocket. I sat alone there, deep in the forest, with men whose sense of right and justice had been outraged to the breaking point. They did not even say goodbye to me at the railroad station. ■ ■

"HUNTING THE PRONG-HORN ANTELOPE"

Seventy-five years ago the little prong-horn antelope was a common sight on our western prairie. From the flat lands of Kansas to the Pacific, from Canada down into Mexico it roamed the feeding grounds outnumbered only by the bison. The latter was singled out by man for wanton slaughter and almost complete extinction while the prong-horn found safety in its size and was overlooked for the larger game to be had. The time came, however, when the bison, wave upon wave of deep brown, ever surging like restless seas across the plains, was to be seen no longer. Men's eyes roamed from north to south in their never-ending desire to wrest still more from the land and their search beheld the prong-horn, now grown big in numbers beside the bison. They, like the bison before them, gazed with curious eyes at man's approach and did not realize that their days were also numbered. Not many years were to pass before they, too, were to be seen in widely separated areas and only upon infrequent occasions.

The true sportsman is not a ravager of game or resources, and the antelope provided him with all the thrills in the hunting that he could wish for. The finest of antelope hunting was to be found in Southern California where the true element of sportsmanship was practiced in chasing down the animal. Looking east from the San Gabriel Mountains lay the great Mojave Desert which abounded with the prong-horn. Because of the treacherous terrain the chase on horse gave the hunted a chance for life and the hunter required excellent marksmanship and horsemanship. The antelope, exceedingly fleet, was able to lead any horse a merry race but, unfortunately, could not endure long stretches because of its delicate leg structure.

Remington's illustration, "Hunting the Prong-Horn Antelope in

153

HUNTING THE PRONG-HORN ANTELOPE IN CALIFORNIA

California" depicts such a chase. The horseman found it necessary to draw abreast of the animal before shooting it. Any attempt to shoot it from behind was practically out of the question since the terrain over which it traveled was awash with gullies and strewn with boulders. This illustration appeared on the cover of *Harper's Weekly*, February 2, 1889 to accompany a story by C. F. Holder entitled "The American Antelope."

In 1889 there appeared a portfolio of color lithograph prints published by Gould, two of the group being by Remington. These were the first Remington prints to be published and oddly were sporting in nature, not western. One of these was entitled "Antelope Hunting." The hunter is shown after his quarry on the western plain where the rise and fall of the land make it necessary for the sportsman to partially stalk his game. The antelope has keen eyesight and is off at the first sign of warning. He has a peculiar trait in that he runs in a direct line and rarely deviates to right or left. If the hunter fails in the stalking he must resort to his horse and meet the game at a focal point some distance away. Another peculiarity of the antelope is his intense curiosity which is often his downfall since he will as likely as not stop suddenly in his mad flight to see if he can discover the cause for his being aroused.

"A GOOD DAY'S HUNTING IN THE ADIRONDACKS"

This illustration appeared along with an article entitled "The Butchery of Adirondack Deer" by Casper Whitney in *Harper's Weekly*, January 16, 1892. Mr. Whitney had this to say about it. "It is rather hard lines on Mr. Remington, I confess, that the letterpress accompanying his spirited drawing should have so murderous a title. Mr. Remington is too good a sportsman to deserve any Caudle lecture from me on the subject of hunting deer and we may be assured that the group of lucky chaps he has presented for our pleasure have not secured their venison by means of jacking or floating or illegitimate hounding, though they should throw that steel trap into the lake instantly."

155

TROUT FISHING THROUGH THE ICE IN THE CANADIAN WILDERNESS

"TROUT FISHING THROUGH THE ICE"

Mr. Julian Ralph wrote an article on the above subject which appeared in *Harper's Weekly*, March 15, 1890. In his comments about the pros and cons of the hunter's life in this Canadian wilderness or any wilderness which was geographically situated where the bitter cold of winter drove a man to distraction, he devoted a portion of his story to salt pork.

"At first, fried salt pork taken three times a day in a hunter's camp, seems not to deserve the harsh things said and written about it. The open air life, the constant and tremendous exercise of hunting or chopping wood for the fire, the novel surroundings of the forest or camp, all tend to make a man say as hearty a grace over salt pork as he ever did at home before a holiday dinner. Where we were, up the Ottawa in the Canadian wilderness, the pork was all fat, like whale blubber.

"I ate my share seasoned with the comments of Mr. Frederic Remington, the artist, who asserted that he was never without it on his hunting trips, that it was pure carbonaceous food, that it fastened itself to one's ribs like a true friend, and that no man could freeze to death in the same country with this astonishing provender."

HER FIRST MUSKALLONGE

"HER FIRST MUSKALLONGE"

In *Collier's Magazine*, dated March 18, 1905, there appeared an article written by Charles B. Davis entitled "Remington—The Man and His Work." An excerpt from this article is quoted:

"His greatest admirer must search in vain through all the artist's pictures and bronzes for a petticoat. The pretty schoolmistress from the east, the rough woman from the mining camp with her heart of gold concealed by her brazen finery, the miner's daughter with her sombrero, the quick wit and unerring aim of her ever ready six-shooter—all of which have proven such excellent material in the hands of Bret Harte and Owen Wister, and all other writers and artists of our western life—have been wholly neglected by Remington."

Mr. Davis must certainly have known Mr. Remington on a personal basis or he would not have written the article. I doubt very much if he was greatly familiar with his work. The second picture of Remington's which was accepted for publication by a national periodical portrayed a woman. Of the eleven illustrations by Remington appearing in Elizabeth B. Custer's "Tenting on The Plains" three drawings are of women. Shown here is a drawing of a little lady on her first fishing adventure which appeared in *Harper's Weekly*, October 6, 1888.

159

RUNNING A COYOTE WITH HOUNDS IN SOUTHERN CALIFORNIA

"RUNNING A COYOTE WITH HOUNDS"

As the west opened up and settlers began pouring onto the plains, the sportsmen among them were not long in finding that the flat prairie was ideal for coursing, a method of pursuing wild game that dates back to ancient times. This pursuit of game with dogs, primarily with greyhounds, took hold and spread until it became deeply entrenched as a great American sport. Few were the ranchmen who did not eventually acquire their pack of dogs and take the utmost pride in their behavior in the field. Lonely army outposts had their own packs with which to break the monotony of the soldier's life on the plains. Anything put up was fair game but the favorites were naturally the fleetfooted animals—deer, jacks, and antelope or the predatory coyote and wolf. Even the wild turkey was not overlooked, and indeed, proved to be a bird worthy of the chase.

Theodore Roosevelt was a staunch advocate of coursing and it can be safely said that he experienced all of the thrills that come to one who follows the hounds. In one of his discourses on the sport, he covers the best means suited to subjugate the wolf, scourge of the old west. "The true way to kill wolves is to hunt them with greyhounds on the great plains. Nothing more exciting than this sport can possibly be imagined."

161

"BULL-FIGHTING IN MEXICO"

The bull-fight is steeped in lore and is treated with all the pageantry that the Spanish people love so well and know how to display. To these people the bull-fight is a pastime more than equaling our games of baseball and football. Although to most of us bull-fighting does not fit into our scheme of things as a sport, we cannot overlook the fact that to millions it is.

On June 1, 1889 there appeared a story in *Harper's Weekly* entitled "Bull-fighting In Mexico" by Thomas A. Janvier. Remington made some fine illustrations for this and they are here reproduced. It may be that Mr. Janvier and the publisher liked them so much that they had him illustrate Mr. Janvier's story "The Aztec Treasure-House" which appeared serially in *Harper's Weekly* several years later and was in turn published in book form, now a must in any collection of Remington's work.

EL CAPEADOR—THE BANDERILLERO'S PLAY

EL PICADOR

THE PICADOR RECEIVING A CHARGE OF THE BULL

A CHULILLO IN TROUBLE

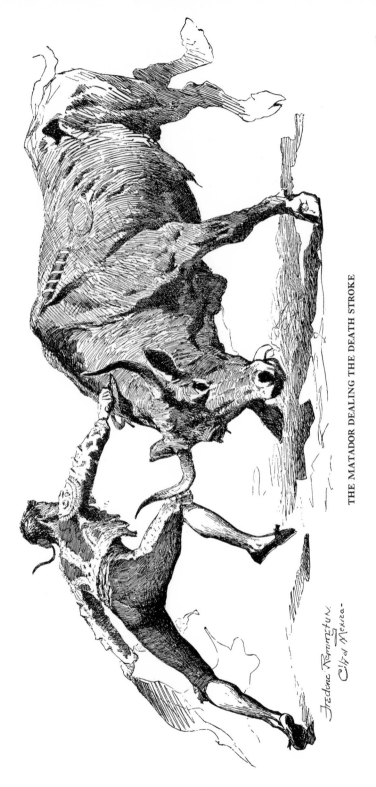

THE MATADOR DEALING THE DEATH STROKE

Remington on Tiger Hunting*

A CHARACTERISTIC STORY IS TOLD of the late Frederic Remington, the distinguished illustrator and sculptor, who also possessed marked ability as a writer. Besides being an admirable companion, with an inexhaustible fund of adventure and anecdote, he had a remarkable faculty for visualizing his experiences in his verbal descriptions.

One day the big genial artist was seated with a number of friends at the general table of a certain club, when the conversation turned upon various kinds of hunting. In the company was a short English army officer on his way through America to an Australian post. It was not long after the topic had been introduced that Remington, after talking enthusiastically of the kinds of sport, reached the climax in tiger-hunting.

"Oh, but the very best of all," he said, "must be tiger-hunting in India. Just imagine the experience," he continued, launching into a description of the sport as he had read of it, and getting more excited as he proceeded, emphasizing his words by descriptive gestures, which added to the enjoyment of his audience. "You see, it's this way. You go out into the edge of the jungle, all mounted on elephants, and fully equipped and just thrilling with anticipation; then you get down and go into the jungle while the beaters are scaring up the game. As you stand there all agog, it must be terribly exciting, every nerve and muscle on strain, and your eyes peering

* S. Walter Jones, "Remington on Tiger Hunting." *Century Illustrated Monthly Magazine,* April 1913.

anxiously into the dim forest." Here Remington wobbled an imaginary rifle, to correspond with the excitement of his voice. "Pretty soon you hear shouts, and a thrashing through the bushes. First thing you know—whist! before you can pull a trigger—a black and yellow streak goes past your head and disappears on the other side, with no chance for you to fire. The beaters come following along, and dash in after the tiger. There you stand more excited than ever. After what seems an eternity, come more shouts and confusion, and excitement, and crash through the bushes comes the tiger again, and streaks past your head, and there you stand as if you had never fired a gun in your life."

Remington's voice had now grown louder, and his gestures more emphatic, and everybody in the room was listening. Just at this moment he caught the eye of the little English captain, who did not seem to be sharing the interest which Remington's graphic description had awakened in the company. Suddenly, Remington's voice dropped to an ordinary tone, and he said,

"Captain, have you ever been in India?"

"Oh, yes; oh, yes," said the captain with a decided English accent on the "oh," like the croaking of a small frog.

"Have you ever been tiger-hunting?"

"Oh, yes; oh, yes."

"Have you ever shot any tigers?"

"Oh, yes; oh, yes, about five and twenty."

Remington hesitated a little, but recovered himself, and went on earnestly:

"Well, captain, isn't tiger shooting as I've described it? Isn't it awfully thrilling and exciting and demoralizing? Don't they come leaping at you?"

"Oh, yes," said the little captain in something above a whisper; "They do bound about a bit." ■ ■

A Gallery of
Sporting Illustrations

JEREMI WAS TOO QUICK WITH HIS GUN

CARIBOU IN SIGHT

175

SOME NOTES FROM LIFE

176

IN A STIFF CURRENT

177

MOOSE HUNTING—AN UNEXPECTED SHOT

179

HUNTING THE MOOSE

CALLING THE MOOSE

182

A WOUNDED BULL ELK

SHOOTING GEESE

HIS BAG

WINTER PASTIMES AT AN ARMY POST IN THE SOUTHWEST— A RUN WITH THE HOUNDS

TARPON FISHING IN FLORIDA—THE JUMP

SPRING FISHING IN CANADA—A GOOD DAY'S SPORT

SPRING TROUT FISHING IN THE ADIRONDACKS – AN ODIOUS COMPARISON OF WEIGHTS